BRISTOL

BULLETS, BLADES AND BARRICADES

PUBLISHED BY BANQUO BOOKS

BRISTOL

BULLETS, BLADES AND BARRICADES

MARK BRIDGEMAN

PUBLISHED BY BANQUO BOOKS

First published in 2025 by
Mark Bridgeman

British Library Cataloguing-in-Publication Data
A catalogue record for this book is available
from the British Library

ISBN 978-1-8381882-5-2

FSC
www.fsc.org
MIX
Paper | Supporting
responsible forestry
FSC® C018072

Printed and bound by Clays Ltd, Elcograf, S.p.A

Published by Banquo Books

CONTENTS

INTRODUCTION

> "For a long time I could not conceive how one man could go forth to murder his fellow, or even why there were laws and governments; but when I heard details of vice and bloodshed, my wonder ceased, and I turned away with disgust and loathing."
>
> Frankenstein, by Mary Shelley

A sense of injustice and anger courses keenly through the blood of Bristolians. In fact, much blood has been spilt in the name of inequality, discrimination, revenge, retribution, jealousy, and greed – to name but a few driving factors. For the noblest and most selfless of reasons, to motives of the darkest and most dangerous kind, *Bristol: Bullets, Blades, and Barricades*, takes you on a journey through some of the murky and murderous chapters in Bristol's history.

Featured among the stories are some of the vilest and most gruesome murders from the city's past, including some recently discovered new material, offering possible solutions to previously unsolved crimes. Any reflection on Bristol's violent past would not be complete without a journey through just some of the riots to that have taken place on the city's streets. On each occasion I have attempted to place the reader on street level, among the baying mob, almost dodging the flying bricks.

Equally, in-amongst the stories of murder, the reader will take their place in the public gallery at a series of some of the most shocking and grisly High Court trials in the city's history. From the case of the body under the floorboards, to the mysterious vanishing wife murderer, the darker side of Bristol's past is contained within these pages.

Not all criminals and murderers are masterminds, as you will discover. Many suffered almost as much as their victims. Perhaps, in a city with a keen sense of justice, there is some comfort in that.

Mark Bridgeman
www.markbridgemanauthor.co.uk

THE PORTWAY TAXI-CAB MURDER (PART ONE)

In the early hours of Wednesday 6th August 1947, Joseph Goessens, a lock gateman at Avonmouth Docks, was cycling home from a late work shift along a quiet stretch of the Portway (the road linking Avonmouth Docks and Avon Gorge with the centre of Bristol). As he rounded a bend in the road he noticed a black-and-white taxi-cab parked at an unusual angle in the middle of the carriageway, along a lonely stretch of the road. Although the time was close to 3am, the waning full moon still provided Joseph with enough light to illuminate the vehicle in front of him. Although it was not unusual to see taxis, at all hours of the day and night, ferrying merchant sailors to and from their vessels at the Avonmouth Docks, this particular cab caught the gateman's attention. As he pulled alongside the vehicle, Goessens noticed that the taxi's starting handle was sitting in the crank position, yet there was no one close by, and the cab, at first glance, appeared to be unoccupied.

Suddenly a young, slim man appeared from the shadows and flagged Goessens down. In a thick Irish accent, the man asked Goessens to help him push the taxi-cab to the verge at the side of the road. Goessens would later make a statement to the Bristol police, describing what happened next.

'He wanted me to help him turn a car around and push it, because he couldn't start it,' the gateman explained. 'It appeared to me that the man did not know what make the car was, because he asked me if I knew how to start a Morris car when the taxi was actually an Austin. It was pitch black at the time and the taxi's headlights were dim. The man did not even know how much petrol there was in the vehicle. Then I noticed, slumped down in the front of the taxi, in a dazed condition, was another man. I thought he was drunk or asleep. The first man and I pushed the car for about fifty yards, and then I opened the driver's door and pulled the hand brake on. I could still see the other man in the front passenger seat; he looked very drunk to me. It was too dark to see anything else though. I was there helping for about twenty minutes, but I made an excuse to get away as soon as I could, 'cause I thought the car was stolen. I asked the man with the Irish accent what the time was. He looked at his watch, and said it was 3:20am. I cycled to the nearest police station at Brandon Hill, and told the officer on duty what had happened.'

After reporting the incident to the police, Mr Goessens then returned to his home in Ashton Gate, while two constables from Brandon Hill station were despatched to the scene. On arrival they were surprised to find the taxi still there, having assumed that the strange affair had been merely a bungled attempt to steal the vehicle. As the two constables approached the vehicle, the first glimmer of dawn was illuminating the gorge. They jotted down the vehicle's registration number in their pocketbooks – 'EHU 232'. The officers also noticed that the starting handle was still in its crank position and removed it carefully with a handkerchief in case any fingerprints might remain. Cautiously shining their flashlights through the passenger window, they could clearly see the unconscious man still slumped in the front seat of the car. However, the unidentified man with the Irish accent who had asked Joseph Goessens for help was nowhere to be seen.

One of the police officers opened the rear door of the

taxi-cab and there, sprawled in the shadowy footwells in the rear of the cab, was another body – that of the taxi driver, William John Herbert Delong. His face and body were badly bloodied, his legs on the seats, and his upper torso and head wedged and twisted in the footwells. He appeared to have passed away recently – probably within the last two or three hours, the constables thought – as the body was not yet cold.

Superintendent Fred Carter, the head of Bristol C.I.D., was hastily recalled from his fishing holiday to head up the murder enquiry. After inspecting the crime scene, he made an announcement to the press:

'Gentleman of the press – this is murder! Mr Delong was a night taxi-cab driver, who lived in Luckwell Road, Bedminster. He was married with three children and has been a taxi driver since last Christmas, when he was demobbed from the R.A.S.C.

A man who was found in the front seat of the cab has been taken to the police station for questioning. At this stage, we do not think this man knew that Mr Delong was dead; however, we do believe that he can give us some valuable information.

No weapons have been found and, at present, we believe robbery to be the motive. It is possible that Mr Delong was working on the engine when he was attacked. Evidently, he put up a big fight, as his body was badly battered.'

The following day, twenty detectives painstakingly cut away the riverbank grass with scythes and poked the undergrowth with sticks, as they conducted a fine-toothcomb search of the ground alongside the Portway where Mr Delong's body and his taxi-cab had been found. After several hours of meticulously examining the area, detectives made a shocking and surprising discovery. Approximately a mile from the scene of Mr Delong's murder, at Lower High Street in Shirehampton, the police found another body, that of a Chinese seaman. He was identified as Fai Kai, a forty-nine-year-old cook serving on the steamship *Newton D. Baker*, currently docked at Avonmouth. Kai was alive, but unconscious and seriously injured. He appeared to have suffered severe facial injuries from a vicious assault, which seemed to display many of the characteristics of the attack on Mr Delong. Kai was transferred to Bristol Royal Infirmary, where he remained unconscious and unable to help the police any further.

Meanwhile, Delong's fellow Bristol taxi drivers were questioned by detectives, and shown photographs of the vehicle, in the hope that they might be able to shed some light on the mystery. One driver noticed that the master switch in Delong's Austin taxi-cab had been switched to the 'OFF' position. Had Mr Delong manually switched the engine off, before his killer or killers, had battered him to death? If so, why? At any rate, detectives speculated, this seemed to indicate that his assailant or assailants possessed little mechanical knowledge, or familiarity with that type of vehicle, since they might have easily restarted the vehicle by returning the master switch to its 'ON' position, rather than placing the starting handle in the crank position.

Another taxi driver also mentioned two particular women, who frequently hired cabs in the Bristol area at night; 'usually with male friends, and they often asked for Mr Delong to drive them. One was a pretty redhead, and the other a brunette with a red coat.'

As the daily cycle of ships due to leave Avonmouth docks continued, officers from Bristol C.I.D. were on hand to question seamen before their vessels departed for international waters. Detective Supt. Carter's initial theory was that the taxi driver had been violently attacked and robbed by several men (possibly sailors) several miles from where the body was found, that he was then bundled into his cab, and driven to a lonely spot on the Portway. Perhaps, it was surmised by Supt. Carter, the Chinese seaman Fai Kai had also been targeted in a similar way.

As public outrage grew in Bristol, four seemingly significant leads soon presented themselves to the under-pressure detectives. Firstly, the police received an anonymous blank postcard addressed simply to 'The Chief of Bristol Police.' The postcard bore no return address, only the words 'I know' written in pencil. Was the postcard a taunt from the murderer of Mr Delong? If, indeed, it was linked to the case at all? Officers kept the postcard as evidence, on the off chance that this small sample of handwriting could be used at a later stage to rule a suspect in, or out, of the investigation.

Secondly, detectives discovered that a tall New Zealander, probably a seaman, had hired Mr Delong's taxi to drive him from Bristol to London just forty-eight hours before his murder. Several witnesses had overheard a disagreement between the two men over the agreed fare for the journey. Had an argument between the two men turned to violence? Detectives were despatched to the capital to search all hostels, cafes, and public houses in the London docks area. Supt. Carter even theorised that perhaps the initial witness Joseph Goessens had been confused, and the man he helped to push the taxi-cab was in fact a New Zealander and not Irish at all. Ultimately, however, the lead would prove fruitless. The tall sailor from New Zealand was never traced.

The murdered man's clothing on the night of his killing also presented the authorities with another puzzling clue. Why, on the very day of his death, had Mr Delong purchased an expensive new suit, and then chosen to wear it while driving on his nightshift, rather than wearing his normal working clothes? It seemed out of character; but was it relevant to the investigation?

Perhaps the most interesting development was the discovery that Mr Delong had picked up two young women – one of whom was described as 'redheaded' – from a Bristol taxi rank at approximately 11pm on Tuesday 5th August, just hours before his death. Were these the two women mentioned by Mr Delong's fellow taxi drivers?

While detectives waited to question the unidentified, supposedly drunk and unconscious man who had been found in the taxi-cab's passenger seat, and was being cared for in Bristol Royal Infirmary, they patiently pieced together a timeline for the evening of Mr Delong's murder. According to the taxi company's docket, Delong had started his night shift at approximately 7:30pm with exactly eight gallons in his petrol tank. Fuel was still strictly rationed at the time and careful records were maintained by taxi firms. Different regulations applied to vehicles approved for commercial use (such as taxis), to those registered for private use. Black market infringements were frequent at the time, with theft of fuel designated for commercial use a regular occurrence, and even a possible motive for Mr Delong's murder. In fact, within a year of this case, the government would introduce the Motor Spirit (Regulation) Act 1948, enforcing the addition of a red dye to petrol designated for commercial use. Any private car owner then found using 'red petrol' in his car would immediately lose his licence.

Returning to the investigation, detectives were notified by an eyewitness that Mr Delong had been seen with his taxi-cab at approximately 10pm on the night prior to his murder at the Temple Meads Station incline. Having picked up a fare from the station, he was then witnessed driving in the Knowle area between 10:10pm and 10:20pm. By 10:25pm he was seen waiting in the taxi rank opposite the Bristol Hippodrome.

At approximately 10:30pm, he left there, apparently heading towards Prince Street carrying a party of three adults and two children. Police were unable to trace this party. However, at 11pm, the attendant at The Grove filling station in the centre of Bristol served petrol to a taxi-cab driver with two young women in his cab. The attendant was adamant that the driver was Mr Delong. This puzzled the investigating officers. If Delong's taxi-cab had at least eight gallons in it at the start of his shift, how could he have possibly used it all by 11pm? Yet the attendant at the Grove filling station was certain that the driver was Delong.

Another witness came forward claiming that they had seen the same taxi-cab parked in Portway at 11:30pm, more than three hours before Mr Goessens had cycled past at approximately 3am in the early hours of the next morning. Assuming that Mr Delong's body was already in the vehicle by the time it was abandoned in Portway, then he must have been killed sometime between 11:30pm on Tuesday 5th August and 3am the following morning. This gave the police an important window. If they could trace both the taxi-cab's movements and passengers between being spotted at The Grove filling station at 11pm, and its appearance in Portway at 11:30pm, it might lead them to Mr Delong's murderer.

A surprise announcement was made on 16th August, when Supt. Carter issued a statement saying that an unnamed man had been arrested. Was this man the person found in the passenger seat of the taxi, who had since been recovering in hospital from the effects of alcohol? Had he regained consciousness and admitted to the murder of Mr Delong? The eager reporters would have to wait a little while longer for their answers; this unidentified man was released without charge two days later.

Finally, on 20th August, Supt. Carter was given permission

by doctors to interview the man recovering in hospital from the effects of alcohol. He identified himself as Mr Owen Cooney, the chief radio officer of the *Coriantes,* currently docked at Avonmouth. An Irishman from Cork, he told detectives that he had begun drinking with a fellow Irishman he had met called John Dillon, a widow named Elsie Bowden (who would later be described by the prosecution as being 'of bad moral character'), and a girl called Ruth, who Cooney described as 'pretty and a redhead'. An examination of Cooney by doctors had revealed that 'his blood showed such a high level of alcohol poisoning that he was lucky to be alive and must have been very nearly in a state of coma when Delong died.' This seemed to rule out Cooney as a suspect in Mr Delong's murder. Nevertheless, his evidence would prove crucial.

'I drank beer and whisky with John Dillon that night,' Cooney confessed. 'I remember drinking till about 9:30pm, the night before the taxi driver died, but my mind became a blank after that, until I found myself with the murdered man in his taxi five hours later. I was in the front seat of the cab when I woke about 2:50am on August 6th. I saw a man in the rear of the taxi, but I didn't examine him. Next, I tried, and failed, to start the engine. I couldn't see Dillon anywhere, so I waited until someone came along. I must have passed out again after that. I don't remember anything else.'

This gave Supt. Carter a strong suspect, John Dillon, and a warrant was issued for his arrest. Despite Dillon being of no fixed abode, he was quickly located and arrested. Under intense questioning by Bristol C.I.D., Dillon would make a statement which he later both denied and retracted:

'I belong to the Animal Gang in Dublin, and we are a lot of tough boys. This is the first murder that I've done though. My head made me do it. Don't know what my old mother will say. I haven't seen a priest for a long while, and I want a confession.

I hired Delong's taxi after meeting two girls named Ruth and Elsie. I then asked Delong to stop by some woods. I had no money. The women had money though, but they would not pay him. An argument started between Delong and myself. I meant to just hit him so that I only knocked him out. I laid Delong on the pavement and told the women to take his money from him. They took some banknotes from his inside pocket, and then they dragged him into the cab and left him in the rear of the vehicle.'

The statement seemed to be damning indeed. One of the two women named by Cooney and Dillon, Elsie Bowden, was also interviewed. Although dismissed by the police at the time as 'little more than a prostitute', her testimony certainly gave the authorities enough evidence to charge Dillon with Mr Delong's murder.

'The two men got out of the cab and started fighting,' Elsie claimed. 'I saw Dillon hit Delong on the head with his fist and Delong said to him, "What's your bloody game?". Dillon then kicked Delong in the stomach while he was on the ground. I left with Ruth and we got a lift back to Bristol in a lorry. Dillon told us to take the taximan's money because he loved me and wanted to use it to marry me.'

John Dillon strongly denied Elsie Bowden's version of events, claiming that, 'The confession I made earlier is untrue, I had nothing to do with the death of Delong. I deny fighting him or even knowing him. I was not in the taxi. It is all lies said by a brainless prostitute.'

Despite Dillon's protestations, he was formally charged with William Delong's murder and remanded to await trial. However, due to his unpredictable state and erratic behaviour, it was decided to keep him under secure observation at Bristol Mental Hospital until his trial. Dillon's wife was brought

over from Dublin to visit and legal representation was found for the accused man, the aptly named Mr F. C. Counsell, Solicitor.

The trial date was set for 19th November at the Bristol Assizes, and Lord Chief Justice Goddard would preside. In the meantime, Delong's fellow Bristol cabbies organised a collection for the murdered man's widow, and provided a cortège of taxi-cabs to escort the hearse to his funeral.

John Dillon's trial opened to a packed public gallery, and he was formally charged with William Delong's murder. Dillon pleaded 'Not guilty'. However, the Crown's advocate, Mr G.D. Roberts K.C., who had recently returned from prosecuting on behalf of the army at the Nuremberg War Trials, had a degree of celebrity and gravitas attached to his name. 'Khaki Roberts' – as he had become affectionately known – would certainly be a formidable opponent for the defence.

The prosecution's case seemed a strong one. It was asserted by Mr Roberts that, 'The killing of Mr Delong had been a premediated one. Why else would they have picked such a lonely and unobserved spot to murder him? The victim's injuries were multiple and severe, ruling out a single, spur of the moment punch as the cause of death in this case. Mr Delong was a thick-set, powerful, muscular man, and it follows that his assailant must have also been a strong man, perfectly capable of inflicting such acute injuries upon a fellow human being.

The medical evidence from Professor James Webster, Director of the Home Office Laboratory no less, corroborates this – and I quote – "This man died from shock due to multiple injuries, distributed mainly over the head, face and neck. Those injuries had been caused by excessive violence, and had been inflicted by a blunt instrument, not excluding, and quite possibly both, the fists and feet of his assailant." The Crown will be providing a string of witnesses to prove, beyond any doubt, that the accused man intended to commit robbery and the foulest of murders on that fateful night.'

The courtroom fell into a state of hushed anticipation as the first witness was called.

THE PORTWAY TAXI-CAB MURDER (PART TWO)

The man who reported his suspicions to the police on the night of the murder, Joseph Goessens, was then called by the prosecution and took his place in the witness box.

'I was cycling across Sea Mills railway bridge when I saw the lights of a car about 150 yards down the road towards Bristol. As I passed the car a man appeared in the middle of the road and signalled me to stop. I spoke to him, I didn't know who it was then, but I now know him to be Mr Dillon. After helping him push the car for a distance of about 50 yards I left him there and cycled to Brandon Hill police station, where I made a statement to the police. I had formed the opinion that the car was stolen.'

'Thank you, Mr Goessens,' said Mr Roberts, 'The prosecution now calls Mrs Emily Bowden.'

'Every time Mr Delong saw me,' she began, 'he used to give me lifts in his cab. On the night he died he was struck on the head by Dillon and the two men then started to fight. Dillon hit Delong again and put his boot into Delong's stomach. I went through his pockets and took £2, and then we picked him up and put him in the back of his cab.'

'Was Mr Delong alive or dead at that point, Mrs Bowden?' asked Mr Roberts.

'I didn't take much notice.'

Lord Goddard interjected at that point to ask the witness a question of his own. 'What about the statement you originally

made to the police in which you said you were elsewhere on that night?'

'That was untrue, your honour. I said that because Dillon said if I split on him he would do me in.'

Constable Arthur Parfitt from Brandon Hill police station was then called to the witness box by Mr Roberts K.C.. 'Constable, please tell the court what you found when you reached the scene of the crime early on that Wednesday morning.'

'Yes, sir,' replied the constable. 'Together with Inspector Culpin, I went to the spot indicated by the previous witness. When we arrived it was about 4:10am and we saw Mr Cooney first in the front passenger seat. He was in a state of intoxication. I examined the car. When I opened the off-side rear door I saw the body of another man, Mr Delong, with bloodstains on his face. Inspector Culpin made an extensive search of the vicinity. He found a pound note in the middle of the road, a set of lower dentures, and a sixpence beneath the body. There was also grass seed in the victim's hair.'

'A set of lower dentures, constable?'

'Yes sir. There was no corresponding set in the mouth of the victim, so we took them to be his.'

'Thank you. And what did you do then, constable?'

'After the body was taken to the city mortuary, we examined the cab of the taxi. There were no signs of a struggle inside the cab, but we did find the bowl of a broken pipe on the driver's side running board. The meter registered a fare of seven shillings and sixpence, but I could not tell if the flag was up or down.'

'Thank you, constable. I understand that you also had an earlier encounter that night with the accused man, Mr John Dillon, just three hours prior to being called out?'

'Yes, sir. At 12:25am I was examining a lorry parked in Prince Street. Inside I saw the accused man asleep, in his stockinged feet. A pair of Wellington boots lay beside him. I ordered him out of the lorry and asked for his identity card, which he produced. I then directed him to a place of shelter – the Salvation Army Hostel.'

'And had you seen Mr Dillon on any other occasion?'

'Yes, sir. About a week previous, in the same lorry. On that occasion he was with one of the other witnesses here today, Mrs Elsie Bowden.'

Next came the evidence of the police officer who had apprehended Dillon a few days later, Detective Sergeant Albert Harris.

'I saw the prisoner in Colston Street,' he informed the court, 'and asked him to come to the police headquarters for questioning in connection with the murder of Mr Delong. He was with Mrs Elsie Bowden at the time, and as he got into the police car she said to him, "Mind you use your loaf." He was then taken to Bridewell Street station and asked to give an account of his movements. The accused man then made a statement to me, which I can read now to the court:

"I did not know the driver before, but I got to know him through Ruth. She called him Bill Delong. I often journeyed in his cab with her. I might as well tell you; I was in the cab that night and I have worried about it ever since. I don't know what Ruth will say when she knows I've told you."

I then cautioned him, but he continued with his statement.

"Paddy hadn't got any money, and Paddy and Bill Delong got arguing and fighting. Paddy got rough with him when he was on the ground."

I asked him who Paddy was and he replied, 'Well, actually, I'm Paddy. It's me you're looking for. I am the murderer."

I cautioned him again, but he continued, "Me, Ruth, and Elsie caught Delong's taxi from the centre to Sea Mills. Before we got to Sea Mills, I asked him to stop. Delong said he wanted the fare, which came to about thirty shillings. I had no money, the women had money but wouldn't pay him. An argument started and I meant to hit him to knock him out, that's all. When he was on the ground I told the girls to take all the money from his pocket. We then put him in the rear of the cab and got a lift in a lorry back into the centre. We slept the night in the waiting room at the station. I told the girls to share out the money so as to take away the suspicion of one of us suddenly having a lot of money."

He then asked to go to the lavatory,' Sergeant Harris continued. 'When he came back he agreed to sign the statement, after which he added,

"It was my head which made me do it. I was put out of the army because of my head."

The accused man then asked me a question, "What do they do with a man who does a murder but is mental?"

I replied that I was in no position to discuss the matter with him.'

'Thank you, Sergeant Harris,' Mr Roberts said, 'and what happened next?'

'I then received instructions to take Dillon to Stapleton Institution. The Mental Hospital is in an adjoining building there. While we were waiting to be let in there, Dillon said to me:

"It is not fair, me going to prison. Ruth and Elsie ought to be there as well."

Then he was admitted for observation. I told the officials at Stapleton that Dillon had been charged under Section 15 of the *Lunacy Act 1890.* I was not present when he was examined by the doctors.'

'Very well. Thank you, sergeant.'

Next to be called to the stand was the imposing figure of Chief Inspector Melbourne Phillips of the Bristol C.I.D., who related his own conversation with Dillon to the court.

'I explained the seriousness of his confessions to him, to which he replied, "Yes, I know. It's my head that made me do it." He then tapped his forehead with his finger and continued, "I am not right up there, you know."

I then asked him the following questions:

What else besides money was taken from Mr Delong? He answered, "A cigarette case that I broke up and threw away because it was dangerous to have it on me."

What happened to Delong's peak cap?

"I burnt it in the wood at Sea Mills," he answered.

Why did you turn the taxi around to face towards Bristol before leaving it?

"I did it as a disguise."

I then informed the accused man that Delong did not have a cigarette case, he was never wearing a peak cap, and that the taxi was found facing Avonmouth and not Bristol. He then asked me:

"Why did you tell me these untruths then?"

Dillon then paused for a moment and told me, "I want to change my statement. I made it up. It's all lies about me being in the car. I knew nothing about the murder. It is my head that makes me say these things."

It was then that we arranged for him to be taken to Bristol Mental Hospital.'

'Thank you, Chief Inspector. And what was the result of the examination at the hospital?'

'The authorities at the hospital regarded him as being perfectly sane, and it was on that basis that I proposed that he be charged with murder. I acquainted him with the statement made by Mrs Elsie Bowden, in which she claimed that he had attacked the driver. He denied it again, and said:

"It is a pack of lies. That damn woman must be mad. I never knew the man who was murdered."

He then made another statement denying any connection between him and the murder and retracting his previous confession.'

The final witness called for the prosecution was a labourer named Percy Cook, from Filton. Mr Cook testified to meeting the accused man on two occasions. 'I first met Dillon after the taxi driver had been murdered, but before he had been arrested. He came up to me and said, "Pop, do you think I am the sort of man who would commit a murder?" I met him again on the day of Delong's funeral, when he said to me, "Pop, I am happy today. They are burying the fool today. Now they can't do anything to me, can they?" That was the last I saw him.'

That concluded the evidence for the Crown, and it was now time for the defence to present their case. Mr C.F. Ingle, Dillon's defence barrister, began by recalling Chief Inspector Phillips to the box, 'I put it to you, Chief Inspector, that you asked my client trick questions, in order to extract a confession.'

'I do not like the word "trick". I only asked certain questions to check the validity of his statement.'

'And did you prompt my client by telling him that if he made certain statements he might only be convicted of manslaughter?'

'No, I did not.'

'But, you were very anxious to make an arrest?'

'Certainly I was.'

'Is it true that the Bristol police have not been successful in one or two cases recently?'

'I don't agree that we have not been very successful.'

'Have you made an arrest in the Odeon murder case, then?'

'No.'

Feeling that he had mortally wounded the prosecution's case, Mr Ingle returned to the matter at hand. 'Very well, and is it true that you were practically certain that the defendant was of unsound mind when first taken to the hospital?'

'Yes.'

'And did the first doctor to examine him not agree with that conclusion?'

'Yes, but the last doctor to examine him thought him perfectly sane.'

Mr Ingle then cross-examined Elsie Bowden. 'Mrs Bowden, in your first four statements to the police you did not mention that you and the accused man were in the cab because Dillon threatened to murder you if you told the truth.'

'I told the truth.'

Undaunted, Mr Ingle continued, 'Was it put to you by the police that if you were able to help and tell the same story as Dillon, that would end the matter as far as you were concerned?'

Elsie Bowden did not answer.

Lord Goddard looked at her sternly and warned her, 'You must answer the question.'

'Yes,' she replied reluctantly, looking down at the floor.

Mr Ingle continued, 'So, having been told that by the police, you made yet another statement, a fifth one I believe, in which you made the accusation against Dillon in connection with the death of the taxi driver?'

'Yes.'

'And you made that statement and are giving this evidence today because you believed the police wanted you to say that?'

'Yes.'

It was now time for the defence to take a huge gamble. John Dillon was called to the stand, in a risky attempt to win the jury's sympathy.

'Mr Dillon,' began his defence barrister, 'please tell the court, in your own words, about yourself and how you were treated by the police.'

'Well, sir, I am married and I have two children. I come from Dublin. We got married in 1942 when I was serving in the Irish National Army. After being discharged a few months later, I joined the British Army and served three years in the Pioneer Corps.'

'Thank you. Tell the court what happened after you were arrested.'

'I was worried and distressed when I was picked up by the police, so I said "yes" to everything they said to me. I was kept in the police station so long that I was nearly falling off my seat because I was half asleep. But they kept bringing me tea to keep me awake. They were questioning me all the time. There was no break. I told them that I had seen Delong with the woman Bowden, but I'd never spoken to him and I had nothing to do with his death.'

In cross-examination, Mr Roberts for the Crown enquired, 'Mr Dillon, you have shown this court considerable knowledge as to how this man met his death, for someone who claims to have not been there. I quote – "I got rough with him when he was on the ground." How do you explain that?'

'I had to say something,' answered the accused man, 'I did not know what I was saying.'

Those were to be the final words uttered by John Dillon, as Mr Ingle brought the defence's case to a close. Both barristers then gave their final summations to the jury.

Mr Roberts, for the prosecution, described the murder as 'brutal and foul' and one for which 'the death penalty is absolutely appropriate.' As the barrister spoke, Dillon leaned against the edge of the dock sobbing and crying.

In his defence's summation Mr Ingle stated that 'All that could be proved was that, following a quarrel, Delong was in a fight with Dillon, who knocked Delong down and, in a temper, kicked him in the stomach. And that the testimony of the prosecution's main witness may be wholly unreliable, since it is served with self-interest, from a woman who the police described as, and I quote, "of bad moral character." I submit, therefore, that this man is not guilty of the murder of Mr Delong.'

The jury was then instructed to retire and consider its verdict. There was a moment of unusual drama to follow, when the foreman of the jury made a highly unusual request to Lord Goddard. The jury, clearly troubled by Mr Dillon's and Elsie Bowden's allegations that they had been 'persuaded' to make their statements by police officers, enquired if further witnesses from the police station could be presented to them to help corroborate the official version of these events. Lord

Goddard refused this request, however, instructing the jury that a decision must be made on the evidence presented. Suitably rebuked, the jury again retired. They emerged an hour later, indicating that they had reached a verdict.

'Members of the jury, have you reached a verdict upon which you all agree?'

'We have.'

'How do you find the defendant, John Dillon?'

'We find him not guilty of murder, but guilty of manslaughter.'

John Dillon collapsed in the dock as the verdict was read out to the court.

The black cap was quietly returned to the clerk's drawer – it would not be needed on this occasion. Lord Goddard then thanked the jury and addressed the prisoner,.

'John Dillon, in passing sentence of twelve years' penal servitude on you, I say this: You may consider yourself a fortunate man. If the jury had found you guilty of robbing this man as well, I would have sentenced you to penal servitude for life. Take the prisoner away.'

John Dillon applied to The Court of Criminal Appeal in May 1949 for an extension in the time allowed for him to lodge an appeal against his conviction. He claimed that his illiteracy prevented him from completing the necessary documentation within the required time period. However, Mr Justice Oliver refused, citing that, 'Dillon was tried for murder, and convicted of manslaughter, and this is one of those cases in which manslaughter approximates very closely to murder. Among the matters Dillon raised was that he was illiterate. Education is not required to realise that the sooner he appeals the better. There are no grounds for extending time.'

Following the failure of his appeal, Dillon served his

remainder of his sentence (less remission) and moved to Camden, London in the mid-1950s. He failed to remain trouble-free, however. After a series of minor offences, he was given a two-year sentence in 1957. Following a conditional discharge he was ordered to report regularly to a probation officer – which he subsequently failed to do. At his hearing in London, Dillon told the magistrate, 'I never realised how serious not reporting is.'

He died in London in 2006 at the age of eighty-three.

Three questions were left unresolved following Dillon's conviction in 1947. Firstly, the nearby attack on the Chinese sailor Fai Kai. Although he recovered, he was never able to name his assailant and the case remains unsolved. Secondly, the true extent of the involvement of the other man, Owen Cooney, and of the two women, Ruth and Elsie, was never fully proved, since their testimony against Dillon enabled the Crown to guarantee at least one conviction in the case. Finally, why – in a move completely out of character – did Mr Delong choose to don a brand-new suit in which to drive his taxi, on the night of his murder, instead of wearing his traditional working clothes? Neither his wife, nor any of the detectives, were ever able to answer this question.

THE BOOK OF SKIN

Housed among the artifacts at Bristol's M Shed Museum is a somewhat macabre exhibit. At first glance it appears to be an old journal, bound in faded brown leather and embossed with a gallows motif. In fact, the nineteenth-century volume is not covered in leather at all. Its binding is constructed entirely of tanned, human skin. The skin of a man convicted of murder. The book itself contains the surviving documentation and letters relating to the tragic death of a young girl more than two centuries ago. While the artifact is wholly genuine, the conviction for murder of the young man, who unwillingly and unknowingly donated his epidermis, may not be.

The string of events which eventually led to the binding in human skin of this rather grisly object began in 1803, in the coalmining community of Hanham, to the east of Bristol. John Horwood had been born into a mining family, the youngest of ten siblings, all raised in an era before the introduction of *1842 Mines and Collieries Act*, which introduced a minimum age of ten for all children forced to work underground. John had little choice and was sent at a tender age to work at one of the several pits in the area. This harsh beginning to a young boy's life seems to have infused him with a sense of bitterness, injustice, and rebellion. After a series of mine accidents and tragedies, including the death of his elder brother, John refused to continue working in the pits. He instead sought employment at the Bristol Brass & Copper Company's spelter works in Hanham. He was soon laid off, however, due to his disruptive behaviour and continued vandalism of company property. Still aged only sixteen, by 1819/20 he had earned an unenviable reputation for harassment, unwanted mischief, and pranks, and for his involvement with a young girl named Eliza Balsam.

John and Eliza had both been born in Hanham during 1803, and had grown up in close proximity. John stated during his later murder trial that he and Eliza had known each other since childhood. According to some sources, they had been involved in a brief relationship which Eliza had ended in 1820, much to the chagrin of the young man. Nevertheless, according to a deposition made by Eliza before her untimely death in 1821 (and reported in the *Bristol Mercury*), their 'relationship' consisted merely of numerous 'improper proposals' to her from the young man. According to Eliza's testimony, 'In consequence of my rejection of him he became very angry with me, and had threatened to murder me.'

At Christmastime in 1820, it was reported that 'Horwood flung a quantity of oil of vitriol (sulphuric acid) or some other deleterious substance over her, which burnt her clothes. After that he repeatedly waylaid her with intent to maltreat her.'

Horwood's harassment of Eliza continued until matters reached a head on Thursday 25th January 1821. Eliza was walking along a country lane near Hanham when she noticed Horwood approaching. Alarmed, and not wishing a confrontation, she turned quickly and ran home. Horwood followed Eliza almost to the door of her family's cottage, and shouted, 'The next time I catch you I'll smash your bones all to pieces.' Unfortunately, for the angry young man, Eliza's mother, Sarah, overheard Horwood's tirade, and demanded to know why he had threatened her daughter. Horwood replied (according to Sarah Balsam's later deposition in court), 'I swear by my maker that I'll kill her, and anyone that takes her part.' He then turned and left.

Just a day later, Sarah Balsam sent her daughter to fetch a pail of water from a small brook in a hollow, at the bottom of a lane in Hanham. Eliza was apparently crossing the brook in the company of two young men, one of whom was allegedly her new sweetheart William Waddy, when John Horwood, who had been stood on the hillside approximately forty yards away, spotted her. Whether one of Eliza's male companions was really her new lover, or merely a friend who had offered to protect her from Horwood's harassment is not known.

Horwood, who was also in the company of two friends – who do not seem to have discouraged him – picked up a stone and hurled it at Eliza, striking her on the right temple and knocking her to the ground in the process. She apparently screamed out, 'Oh Lord, I am killed!' However, according to a different, and far less dramatic version of events, Eliza merely expressed her pity that anyone would do such a thing. Horwood and his companions promptly returned to the village and Eliza walked home clutching her wounded face. No complaint was made to the authorities regarding his behaviour. Indeed, life continued as before for Horwood. For the next week, he remained at his work, and there is no record of him being accused of attempted murder, or even of assault.

Meanwhile, Eliza walked to Bristol Infirmary in Upper Maudlin Street and back, repeatedly over the next few days to have her headwound bathed and dressed; a return journey of some eight or nine miles. That might well have been the end of the story, had the senior surgeon at the Infirmary, Mr Richard Smith, not happened to notice the bandaged Eliza in the waiting-hall at the hospital on the morning of 31st January. Smith, who as the hospital senior surgeon had not attended to Eliza's headwound, happened to pass her as she sat waiting to have her dressing changed. He asked Eliza what had caused the injury, and on receiving the answer, insisted that he observe her wound more carefully, reminding her how serious head injuries can sometimes be. By all accounts, Eliza was reluctant and did not think her injury warranted any further examination. Nevertheless, she was admitted to the hospital for a depressed fracture.

Eliza seems to have responded well initially. However, on 10th February, she appears to have been 'feverish and restless.' Mr Smith called a consultation with his colleagues at the Infirmary, and it was agreed to perform a cranial trephination on the patient. Trepanning, even by early nineteenth century standards, was considered to be an ancient form of neurosurgery in which a circular hole was drilled into the skull in order to relieve pressure or fluid. It was also believed to ward off evil spirits. Following the operation, it was recorded in the medical diaries of Dr Edward Estlin (a contemporary of Smith's), that Eliza's wound was 'greatly infected', and that, 'a small quantity of matter was found between the dura mater and bone, and some relief was at first afforded.'

Sadly, and perhaps not surprisingly, this relief was short lived. Within a few days, Eliza's condition worsened. The surgeon contacted the authorities, informing them of Horwood's attack on Eliza and her resulting injuries. Two burly constables, a sheriff's yeoman, and several members of the public were then sent to detain the young man. The resulting melee in which Horwood strenuously resisted arrest hardly helped his case. Indeed, he seemed to be fully prepared for such a visit, as one of the constables reported:

'The villain guessed our errand, and tried to jump out from a bedroom window in his shirt… he seized a quarryman's hammer, and placing himself on the top of the stairs, threatened, with horrid oaths, the destruction of all who approached. The villain made a great many blows with his hammer. The Officers closed upon him, knocked him down and after a desperate conflict, at last handcuffed him and dragged him to the carriage.'

Following his arrest, Horwood was escorted to the Infirmary and confronted with Eliza so that statements could be taken. She turned her face away from his, refusing to look at 'the villain who had murdered her.' Horwood repudiated her testimony, stating 'I deny murdering her' – a strange defence for someone to make when their victim is still alive. It was noted by the officers that he 'appears to have exhibited but little either of fear for his own fate, or of sympathy with hers.' After the encounter, and by way of a salutary lesson, Horwood was then escorted to the surgeons' consulting-room, and shown the skeletons of two murderers which were displayed there.

Sadly, Eliza died on 17th February 1821, one week after her surgery. A post-mortem recorded the cause of death as 'a cerebral abscess from the injury to her head which was caused by a stone.'

A charge of murder was then brought against John Horwood and a case prepared against him. Finally, on Wednesday 11th April (an unusually long passage of time in 1821 between the execution of the crime and the resulting trial) Horwood's trial took place at The Star Inn in Bedminster. Public houses frequently acted as makeshift courthouses at the time. They tended to offer three distinct advantages over formal public buildings (of which there were few at this time); sufficiently sized public rooms, capable of accommodating a jury, a large table on which the victim's body could be displayed, and the ability to offer both accommodation and refreshment to the visiting magistrates.

The prosecution was fully prepared. The defence, it seems, scarcely made an effort. A phrenological report had been prepared for the Crown by Mary Anne Schimmelpenninck to attempt to prove Horwood›s guilt by the shape of his skull. Schimmelpenninck, a leading writer in the growing anti-slavery movement in Bristol and family friend of Dr Richard Smith, had also developed a system for categorising phrenological characteristics, which would be later published as the *Phrenographic Register.* Her research claimed that, based purely on the shape of Horwood's skull, his chief mental characteristics were 'combativeness', 'self-esteem', and 'hope'. Unfortunately for the prosecution, the 'bump of murder' which was supposedly the crucial cranial characteristic in all murderers, was not present. This flaw in the prosecution's evidence was conveniently overlooked by the jury, and not mentioned by Horwood's defence.

Dr Richard Smith was also called as a witness, and even appeared in the witness box with the top portion of Eliza's damaged skull in his pocket; although good taste seems to have prevented him from producing it in court.

The two crucial stumbling blocks in establishing Horwood's definitive guilt should have been overcome by even a semi-competent defence lawyer. Firstly, his intention to deliberately murder Eliza was not argued. Surely, a single stone thrown from forty yards away seems a singularly poor choice of murder weapon, and Horwood's claim that he acted in anger and meant 'merely to punish her' seems a more likely one. His intent to murder seems problematic. Secondly, the reputation and good character of the surgeon, Richard Smith, carried far more weight during the proceedings than the petulant attitude of the accused man.

Three factors appear to have significantly prejudiced his case: his previous bad character, his earlier threats to Eliza and her mother, and the persistent rumour that he was associated with the infamous 'Cock Road Gang' (a notorious group of villains and robbers who frequented the Blue Bowl Inn in Hanham). However, perhaps the single strangest component lacking in Horwood's defence was the failure to challenge the actual cause of Eliza's death. There is every possible chance that the poor girl's demise was caused by an infection produced by the cranial trephination and that, had she not been hospitalised, she may have recovered as an out-patient. This, at the very least, casts grave doubt over a proven conviction for murder.

John Horwood was clearly a violent and unpleasant young man, but he may not have been guilty of Eliza's murder. Nevertheless, the court had little doubt of Horwood's guilt. He was found guilty of murder and sentenced to death:

'Let him be instantly hanged by the neck until he shall be dead on Friday the 13th April instant.'

Even his young age did not seem to warrant any mitigation in his sentence – Horwood had celebrated his eighteenth birthday on the day preceding his trial.

The convicted man seemed to crumble almost immediately. On the following day he requested that the prison's chaplain, Rev. S. Day, visit him in his cell. After receiving a sermon, Horwood asked that he be allowed to address his fellow prisoners. The *Bristol Mercury* later recorded the events.

'Horwood exhorted them to take warning from him, for that his sins had brought him to his present unhappy condition. He acknowledged that the evidence upon which he had been convicted was true; that he knew it was Eliza Balsam who was passing the brook, and that he was waiting for her at the time. Then, raising his hands and eyes towards heaven, he added, "Lord, thou knowest that I did not mean then to take away her life, but merely to punish her, though I confess I had made my mind, at some time or another, to murder her." He confessed, also, that he had been guilty of several robberies, and said after he had flung the stone, he immediately ran away. On the night prior to his execution the Rev. Mr. Roberts was with him for a long time, and to him said he was not afraid to die, and hoped that tomorrow he should meet the dear girl in heaven.'

He was hanged the following day at Bristol's New Gaol in Spike Island, becoming the first person to be executed at the newly built prison. At 12:50pm Horwood shared a final prayer with the prison chaplain before being escorted to the dead-room under 'the drop', where he remained until 1:05pm, at which point the clergyman left him. At 1:10pm Horwood ascended the platform, and, as he passed the prison warders on the stairs, he kissed each one on the hand, declaring that he bore them no animosity. It was reported that he appeared, 'in firm step, calm and collected.' The executioner removed the condemned man's neckcloth, placed a cotton cap over his eyes, and adjusted the rope. However, the prison governor, Mr Humphries, seemed to be reluctant to drop his handkerchief, the traditional signal to the hangman and to the crowd that the condemned man was about to be 'launched into eternity.' So large was the gathered throng, that posters had been placed outside the gaol warning that any sudden surge might cause spectators to stumble over the bank of the New Cut and drown.

The crowd assumed that the unusual delay was due to prison governor's reluctance in beginning the execution. In fact, the jostling throng of spectators were unable to see that Horwood, from underneath the cotton cap placed over his face, had engaged in deep prayer which lasted almost thirty minutes, after which he made one final request to Mr Humphries,

'Do you think I should have much pain in dying? If I struggle, I wish to be put as quickly out of my misery as possible.'

At 1:30pm the handkerchief was finally dropped and the *Bristol Mercury* noted that Horwood was, 'launched into eternity, in the presence of an immense assembly of spectators. He seemed to die instantaneously. A number of foolish women from the large crowd ascended to the top of the platform after the culprit was turned off, for the purpose of having their disorders cured by touching his dead hand.'

This was not the end of the punishment to be suffered by John Horwood and his family. Under the terms of the *1752 Murder Act*, the body of a convicted killer could not be returned to his family for burial, but instead must be donated to medical science first. The terms of the *Act* were starkly unambiguous.

'In no case whatsoever shall the body of any murderer be suffered to be buried unless such body shall have been dissected and anatomised in the same manner as is now practised for the most atrocious crimes. A penalty will be imposed upon anyone who attempts to evade the directions of the statute.'

Horwood's family and friends appealed to Dr Richard Smith at the Bristol Infirmary for the return of John's body, so that they might afford him a Christian burial. The doctor, who had the first legal claim on the corpse, was a fair man and submitted the claim for consideration at a meeting of senior officials at the hospital. The appeal was refused, however, and amid huge protests he made plans to secretly remove the remains of John Horwood from the gaol. As predicted by the doctor, Horwood's friends hatched a plot to rescue his body as it was taken from Bristol Infirmary for anatomisation, then spirit it away in a boat along the river and back to Hanham. Dr Smith anticipated their plan and instead removed Horwood's corpse by coach during the dead of night; after first issuing the prison's governor with a receipt, to give the impression that the body had already been confiscated. With Horwood's body hidden inside a hackney-coach, he drove up to the Infirmary door, cooly summoned two hospital porters, and hurried the body inside. He noted in his journal that a soldier and a woman passing by, 'glanced curiously at the strange burden, and seemed much astonished; but, fortunately, no one took further notice.'

In order to dissect the organs and display the skeleton, Horwood's skin was first removed. Although in some cases the skin would have been destroyed, Dr Smith, being something of an antiquarian, choose to flay and tan the skin (in full view of eighty medical students) and use it to bind his collections of papers documenting the murder, trial, and execution of John Horwood. He even kept the receipt for the cost of the morbid binding – £1 and ten-shillings, approximately £200 today.

Dr Smith preserved the skeleton at his home until his death in 1843, when it was passed to the Bristol Royal

Infirmary Museum, then to Bristol University. Horwood's skeleton was then kept hanging in a cupboard at the University with the noose still around its neck, until a successful campaign by Mary Halliwell, the great-great-great-granddaughter of Horwood's brother, finally saw him given a proper burial at Christchurch, Hanham, in 2011. Eliza, the forgotten victim in this tragedy, was buried at St Mary's Church in Bitton, Gloucestershire.

The question of John Horwood's guilt for the crime of murder placed a microscope on the harshness of nineteenth-century justice, almost immediately. A campaign for leniency from Horwood's family fell on deaf ears and his execution was almost immediate.

The respectability of a senior surgeon perhaps blinded the court to Dr Smith's anxious desire to have the initial injury, and not the operation, listed as Eliza's cause of death. The medical profession's unquenchable thirst for experimental cadavers may also have played a part in the sad affair.

In September 1869, the *British Medical Journal* carried out a review of the evidence contained in The Book of Skin, and published their conclusions. Less than fifty years after the tragic death of Eliza Balsam, many of the original findings were already being questioned, even by the medical profession.

'The notes of the post-mortem examination do not inform us definitely whether there was an abscess, or any pus, in the arachnoid cavity; but we suppose, from some expressions, that the cause of death was cerebral abscess… A point which impresses one very strongly in this case, is the circumstance that punishment was awarded on account, not of the action and its intent, but of its results. Had the girl recovered, nothing more would have been said about the matter. The unjust apportioning of punishment to results, rather than acts, occurs constantly, but we do not remember to have met so definite an example of it as we have here.'

On the night before his execution, Horwood composed the following poem, which was made public after his hanging:

JOHN HORWOOD IS MY WRETCHED NAME
AND HANHAM GAVE ME BIRTH
MY PREVIOUS TIME HAS BEEN EMPLOYED
IN RIOTING AND MIRTH.
ELIZA, OH ELIZA DEAR!
THY SPIRIT, OH, IS FLED!
AND THY POOR MANGLED BODY LIES
NOW NUMBER'D WITH THE DEAD.
CURS'D IS THE HAND THAT GAVE THE BLOW
AND CURS'D THE FATAL STONE
WHICH MADE THY PRECIOUS LIFE BLOOD FLOW
FOR IT HAS ME UNDONE.

WHEN BRISTOL RIOTED – THREE DAYS IN OCTOBER

"A riot is the language of the unheard."
Martin Luther King, Jr

For three days during October of 1831, it could be argued that England stood closer to the precipice of a class revolution than at any time in its history, either before or since.

Frustrated by the blocking of the second Reform Bill (*The Representation of the People Act*) by an obstinate Tory dominated House of Lords, large throngs of disenchanted and embittered protestors took to the streets of England's cities to demonstrate their frustration. Riots followed in London, Leicester, Yeovil, Sherborne, Exeter, Bath, Nottingham, and Derby. Crucially, matters reached a head on the streets of Bristol from 29th – 31st October, in perhaps the largest and most violent three days of rioting ever witnessed in an English city. Not since the Gordon Riots in London, more than fifty years earlier, had the population of one city stood together so steadfastly to display their anger and frustration at the government of the day. The target of their fury was the injustice felt by the poorer working classes at the rising cost of living and Britain's undemocratic voting system that enfranchised just 5% of the population. Bristol, a city of more than 100,000 people at that time, returned just two Members of Parliament. To make matters worse, the failure of the first and second Reform Bills to pass through the House of Lords seemed to make the dream of a fairer electoral system an even more distant one.

The authorities and the elite ruling classes, still stung by the effect of the French Revolution a generation earlier, prepared for the worst, as buildings were torched and nights of rioting created panic in several cities. Tensions in the country had been slowly increasing since the turn of the century. In August 1831, Bristol's senior judge, Charles Wetherell, spoke in the House of Commons and announced that the people of his city stood resolutely united *against* voting reform (this, despite the fact that a 17,000-signature petition supporting reform had been collected in Bristol and several protests already organised). Privately, the Bristol Corporation feared the worst. Under-Sheriff Hare reported having only one-hundred constables at his disposal. It had been estimated that he would require at least three times that number to control any anticipated rioting.

The government publicly refused Bristol's request for army support, while privately preparing the Dragoon Guards for action. With the Reform Bill having already been defeated twice in the Lords, and Prime Minister Lord Grey resigning, the aldermen of Bristol hoped that their appointment in September of the respected Charles Pinney as mayor of the city would subdue the growing unrest. Pinney was a pro-reform Whig politician, wealthy Bristol merchant, partner in a lucrative West Indies sugar plantation, and president of the Anchor Society (a Bristol charity founded to benefit the people of Bristol and Bath).

Nevertheless, Pinney's actions following his appointment did nothing to placate the rising tensions in the city; in fact, they had the opposite effect.

The aldermen of Bristol firmly believed that Charles Pinney's selection as mayor would be seen by the population as a measure of pro-reform appeasement. However, Pinney, by virtue of his new office as Mayor, was now solely responsible for organising and leading the city's response to the any anticipated unrest. Perhaps unwisely, he chose to take a politically neutral stance in the weeks leading up to the riot. Pinney soon became seen by many as a man who had abandoned his own beliefs (just one year earlier he had been a public supporter of the second French Revolution), with the goal of becoming an establishment figure while simultaneously protecting his vast personal wealth.

It would not be long until tensions in the city boiled over. The announced arrival in Bristol on Friday 29th October of the city's senior judge Charles Wetherell sparked public anger. Worse still, Wetherell – who, just two months earlier had infuriated Bristolians by publicly attaching anti-reform credentials to the city – was scheduled to arrive by carriage for the pomp surrounding the Autumn Assizes, accompanied by none other than Charles Pinney. It does not seem to have occurred to any of the city's aldermen that Wetherell's untimely appearance would almost certainly lead to public agitation and unrest.

The sympathies of Charles Wetherell were obvious to all. He was a noted and vocal opponent of electoral reform. Wetherell was in fact the Member of Parliament for Boroughbridge in Yorkshire, a 'rotten borough' consisting of just forty-eight voters, which would have been abolished had the second reading of the Reform Bill been passed.

On 18th October 1831, a number of military personnel (mainly sailors and anti-reformers) met to discuss the formation of a bodyguard to protect Wetherell on his impending visit. The meeting was broken up by the reform supporting Bristol Political Union (BPU) and violence was narrowly avoided. The BPU had been originally formed as the Bristol General Union of Trades, and represented many of the city workers.

Yet, still, tensions simmered. Six days later, angry pro-reformers protested vigorously at the arrival in Bedminster of the establishment figure George Henry Law, the Bishop of Bath and Wells. Sarcastic and clearly inflammatory billposters were pasted to noticeboards around the city exhorting the citizens of Bristol to'Receive him with every demonstration that becomes his exalted rank, and his LATE VOTE IN THE HOUSE OF LORDS. Refrain therefore from HOOTING, PELTING, GROANING, HISSING or any other annoyance that may be offensive to a man who has so recently declared himself against the VOICE OF THE PEOPLE.'

The Bishop had recently voted against the passage of the second *Reform Bill* in the House of Lords, along with twenty of the twenty-one other Church of England Bishops granted a seat in that chamber. The frustration of the ordinary man seemed to be blocked at every turn by the privileged establishment. Once again, violence was narrowly avoided.

William Herapath, the leader of the BPU, met with city leaders and agreed that his organisation would maintain neutrality and help maintain order on Bristol's streets, on the condition that the army was not mobilised. Despite Herapath's confidence that the BPU was capable of preserving order in the city, the Under-Sheriff attempted to recruit extra volunteers from among Bristol's middle middle-class merchant population (who had previously made themselves available in similar circumstances). Unfortunately, the expected numbers did not materialize, leaving the city with a mere 119 volunteers – many of whom were known to harbour violent tendencies and appeared more likely to inflame rather than extinguish any potential disturbance. Eventually it became clear that armed troops would be needed to quell the growing disorder. City magistrates approached the Home Secretary, William Lamb, who reluctantly deployed a detachment of ninety-three dragoons from the 14th Light and 3rd Guards divisions. This move would only serve to antagonise Bristolians further, particularly the arrival in the city of soldiers from the 14th Light Dragoons. Known as the 'Bloody Blues', they had recently been involved in the heavy-handed suppression of civil disorder in other parts of the West Country.

As news of the Dragoons' impending arrival reached Bristol, magistrates ordered the emptying of all gunsmiths' shops in the city, in case of looting. Tradition demanded that city leaders ride at the head of the troops as they entered the city. However, they refused, for fear that their own business premises would be ransacked or set ablaze.

Wetherell and Pinney's carriage was due to arrive in Bristol on Saturday 29th October. Both men hoped to quell the growing ill-feeling in the city, yet also feared for their own safety. Despite their expected path into the city centre being secretly changed for security reasons, the growing mob quickly became aware of the new route. As it reached Queen Square, the atmosphere among the gathering crowd grew evermore tense and intimidatory. Incensed ringleaders among the mob hurled stones and bricks towards the possession. Wetherell and Pinney, concerned for their own welfare, fled for refuge to the mayor's residence, the Mansion House. Meanwhile, the city's special constables charged the crowd. The heavy-handed approach of the constables surprised even the watching Dragoons, as many protestors fell injured in the resulting melee. The angry crowd responded and many of the volunteer constables abandoned their posts and fled the scene. Twice, Charles Pinney appeared (perhaps unwisely) at the windows of the Mansion House and attempted to calm the situation. However, he could not make his voice heard over the noisy mob and, as nighttime approached, was left with no option but to read the *Riot Act* to the assembled throng. *The Riot Act* of 1714 had been originally introduced during a time of great civil disturbance in Britain, and gave local officials a legal mechanism to order the dispersal by force of 'any group of twelve people or more who were unlawfully, riotously, and tumultuously assembled together'. If the group failed to disperse within one hour, then 'anyone remaining gathered was guilty of a felony without benefit of clergy, punishable by death.' By 1831 the public reading of *The Riot Act* had become more generally utilised by the authorities to issue a stern warning or reprimand, rather than as a precursor to arrests. Interestingly, the saying 'to read the Riot Act' to someone still lives on today, despite its original meaning being long forgotten.

As darkness fell in Queen Square, an angry mob stormed the Mansion House. The 14th Light Dragoons held rank and fired at the crowd, attempting to halt the surge. One man, Stephen Bush, was shot and killed. Meanwhile, Charles Wetherell managed to flee the Mansion House by jumping from the rooftop onto an adjacent building. Somehow, in the resulting confusion, Charles Pinney escaped to Alderman Daniel Fripp's house in Berkeley Square, where he hid for the night and much of the following day. Rioting temporarily subsided overnight. Nevertheless, at first light on Sunday morning, the looting and sacking of the Mansion House continued. Efforts by the small number of Dragoons present to control the rush became hampered by the growing number of middle-class merchants and businessmen, who now appeared to be supporting the rioters, rather than their usual stance of solidarity alongside the authorities. Perhaps they too feared for the security of their own premises.

Meanwhile, inside the Mansion House, the capacious wine cellar was emptied and the building set alight. The rioters, emboldened with alcohol, soon rampaged out of control. From his hiding place in Berkeley Square, Charles Pinney attempted to restore command in the city by ordering a notice to be read out at the city's churches urging local posses of volunteers from the so-called 'respectable classes' to band together and come to the aid of the authorities. However, with city leaders now widely dispersed around the city for their own safety, and limited numbers of willing volunteers, the request failed to allay the spreading riots. Even a small force of soldiers from the Dodington Yeomanry were quickly withdrawn when no city magistrate could be found to issue instructions or requisition lodgings for the men.

William Herapath of the BPU addressed the mob, but to no avail, as confusion and mistrust between the civic and military leaders failed to curb the spread of violence in the city centre. Lieutenant-Colonel Thomas Brereton, in command of the 3rd Dragoons, was forced to dissuade Charles Pinney from issuing a direct order to fire on the mob. Brereton was inexperienced in matters of public order and undoubtedly felt hamstrung by Pinney's ineffective communications, and by previous criticism of the army's heavy-brutal tactics during the Peterloo Massacre in Manchester twelve years earlier.

Yet, conversely, and to the horror of many, the reaction of the over unit of Dragoons, the 14th, to an attack on the newly built Council House in Corn Street, was anything but cautious. Their attack on the large crowd gathered in Corn Street resulted in several injuries and the death of two men. On hearing the news of the assault by the 14th, Lieutenant-Colonel Brereton (who had been placed in overall command of the Dragoons), ordered the 'Bloody Blues' to withdraw from Corn Street to their billet in Keynsham, after an assurance from ringleaders of the mob that they too would disperse. However, hostilities lulled for only a short period, before tempers flared once again.

Fortuitously, this brief cessation in violence did allow Charles Wetherell to escape the city disguised as a woman.

Meanwhile the few remaining soldiers from the 3rd Dragoons, many of whom had pro-reform sympathies, were powerless to stop the escalating disturbances which had now spread from Queen Square to dwellings on Prince Street, King Street, College Green, and to several important municipal buildings. Most ominously of all, rioters stormed Bridewell Gaol, Lawford's Gate Prison, and the Gloucester County Prison. The doors to the prisons were broken down using sledgehammers looted during the previous evening from Acraman's Iron Foundry in Bathurst Basin (this fact was later used as evidence of a degree of premeditation by the rioters). The prison buildings were then overrun, guards fled, and hundreds of prisoners were freed.

Rioters moved in waves from building to building in Queen Square, spreading along Prince Street, Little King Street, and rapidly along both sides of the river. Armed with sticks, iron railings, stones, flaming torches, and tools looted from blacksmiths and ironmongers, the rioters attacked and set light to public buildings including warehouses, the three tollhouses on Prince's Street Bridge, the Wells, and at St Philip. The Customs House, Excise Office, and Bishop's Palace were also targeted. Miraculously, Bristol Cathedral somehow managed to escape any damage. An attempt was then made to storm the city's dock company on the Cumberland Basin and the dock gates were burnt. The crowd chanted 'Down with the churches and mend the roads with them!', and 'It's only corporation property!'. A large mob even taunted the watching Dragoons and officials by openly stating their next target – the city's banks. No symbol of authority seemed safe from the anger and injustice felt by the rapidly moving throng. Such was the scale of the carnage it was reported that the fires could be seen from Newport in Wales, more than thirty miles away.

There seemed to be no let up in the intensity of the destruction. The ransacking and torching of private homes continued during Sunday night and into Monday morning. So shocked were the 'respectable classes' in Bristol that a volunteer force of around 3,000 men reported for duty, anxious to defend their homes and businesses. In addition, a further 100 soldiers from the 14th Light Dragoons arrived in the city on Monday afternoon. Led by two experienced officers, Major Beckwith and Major Mackworth, from the War Office, it soon became clear that the government intended to end the riots quickly. The two officers effectively superseded Lieutenant-Colonel Brereton's authority and ordered a sabre charge on a band of troublemakers rioting on the southern side of Queen Square. Coupled with the increased presence from the volunteer force and the arrival later in the day of General Sir Richard Downes Jackson, accompanied by several hundred armed troops, the riots eventually subsided and the troublemakers either dispersed or were arrested. Only when he felt that control of the streets had been regained, did Under-Sheriff Hare agree to employ 400 members of the BPU to patrol the streets, at the city's expense, paying each man at the rate of three shillings and sixpence a day (approximately £22 today).

With an uneasy peace restored and the riot over, it was now time for Bristol to count the cost.

WHEN BRISTOL RIOTED – THE AFTERMATH AND THE LIST OF SHAME

In the immediate aftermath of the rioting, the city resembled an apocalyptic warzone. A period of Martial Law was invoked and for four long months Bristol was governed by General Jackson and his troops. Large swathes of Bristol had been destroyed by fire. Symbols of authority, such as the mayor's Mansion House, had been razed to the ground, necessitating an extensive rebuild of many buildings in the city centre. It was estimated that damage in the region of £300,000 had been caused by the mob (equivalent to some £40 million today). Eventually, a financial compensation bill agreed to pay each affected household the sum of £500. Together with other costs, a staggering £600,000 would be paid out to the many citizens, business owners, and merchants affected by the riot.

The true number of people killed during the rioting will probably never be established. It is known that twelve members of the public were killed during clashes with the Dragoons, and that a substantial number of bodies were later recovered from the many burnt-out buildings. Total casualties from the riots were traditionally estimated to have been between 125 to 250 people. However, recent research undertaken in 2020 placed the figure at nearer to 500.

Inevitably, the resulting inquiries attempted to establish blame on both sides of the spectrum. Parliament displayed little confidence in Charles Pinney and his leadership. Pinney was tried in 1832 for being 'criminally negligent, due to the ludicrous – had it not been lamentable – inefficiency in the measures taken against the rioters.' After a seven-day trial he was eventually acquitted. He then claimed £2,000 in recompense from the city of Bristol for damage and theft caused during the storming of the Mansion House, and for the financial loss incurred from the looting of his wine cellar.

In the years following the riots, Pinney continued his business operations in Bristol and was awarded £3,572 in compensation for the loss of his slaves following the passing of *The Slavery Abolition Act 1833*. After losing his council seat in 1835, he defected to the Tory party. Pinney passed away in 1867 leaving a fortune of £60,000 (around £8 million today).

Lieutenant-Colonel Thomas Brereton was not so fortunate. He was court-martialled in January 1832 on eleven charges, including that of 'failing to make any effort to arrest the progress of the fire (in Queen Square), or to prevent the plundering and firing of other houses.' He attempted a plea bargain, which was refused, and he took his own life before his trial concluded.

Charles Wetherell's decision to visit Bristol, despite the obvious ill-feeling towards him, was roundly criticised by the press. He was variously described as 'the buffoon of the anti-reform faction' and as having 'dared the hostility' of Bristolians. The *Bristol Mercury* added that Wetherell had arrived in the city with 'the old Tory gang of hired bludgeon-men.'

The rioters themselves did not escape blame either. Allegations and counterclaims were made by both pro and anti-reformers. Multiple allegations were made, ranging from French revolutionary involvement to the claim that members of the Birmingham Political Union had travelled to Bristol to deliberately agitate the population.

The statue of William III in Queen Square was covered with the French tricolour during the riot, no doubt a provocative display of symbolism designed to spread genuine fear of a French style revolution amongst the establishment elite. The *Bristol Gazette* was certain of the rioters' identity, stating the mob 'wholly consisted of boys and striplings, persons evidently without stated employment, which the densely populated purlieus of wretchedness in St Philips and the neighbourhood of Lawford's Gate had sent forth on the occasion', and that many among them 'were women of abandoned character.'

Miners from the Kingswood collieries were also wrongly accused of involvement, despite assurances from the pit owners that 'the men had all turned up for work.'

In fact, the motivations of the Bristol rioters cannot be easily pinned down. Even the breakdown of those involved paints a confusing picture. Under-Sheriff Hare testified that 'The crowd surrounding us was of all classes, respectable, well-dressed people – however, the actual agents of the mischief were the lowest classes.' Another witness claimed that among the crowd, which had gathered on Brandon Hill to shout abuse at the Dragoons, were 'Gentlemen with silk umbrellas over their heads; and the females had silk cloaks and pelisses.'

The riots do not seem to have been chaotic in nature. The majority of buildings targeted were municipal, or homes belonging to wealthy members of the establishment, not the dwellings of ordinary, working families. The protest was, for the most part, targeted only at the slow progress of parliamentary reform, perhaps explaining why many of those convicted for their part in the troubles garnered a great deal of public sympathy.

It was broadly believed among the city's Tories that the riots had been intentionally allowed to grow rapidly out of control, in order that the Whig Government might gain some political advantage by discrediting the local Bristol authority.

The inept response of local officials certainly led to the anger and frustration felt, and no doubt led to the escalation of the drink-fuelled destruction and looting. Yet, the proposed (and twice blocked) measures originally proposed in the Reform Bill would have only extended the franchise to a small proportion of those involved in the disturbances. Although the inadequacies of the voting system at the time were keenly felt, Bristol – with its two members of Parliament – was in fact better represented than many other English cities at that time. Yet, the resentment felt in Britain by the working classes during the first third of the nineteenth century seems to have reached a crescendo in Bristol during those three October days.

The following rarely seen and remarkably comprehensive list detailing those injured in the riots, was published in the

London Packet and New Lloyd's Evening Post. It provides us with an accurate demographic of the protestors involved and of the atmosphere surrounding the city at that time. Indeed, perhaps many modern Bristolians will recognise the surnames listed here, or may even be fortunate enough to trace their ancestry back to the individuals the authorities felt should be 'named and shamed' in such stark and tragic detail:

WEDNESDAY 9TH NOVEMBER 1831
BRISTOL INFIRMARY

> The following is a list of the names of the persons who were injured at the late riots, their places of residence, and a description of their wounds. It may be stated that all the persons at present arrested on the charges of riot and incendiarism are residents of Bristol, though nine out of ten of the latter listed are Irishmen.

OUT CASUALTIES – SABRE WOUNDS,
AND CONTUSIONS FROM THE HORSES.

John Thomson, aged 31, wound of the arm – resident at Bristol.
Cornelius Copley, 34, wound of the arm – Bristol.
Joshua Squires, 52, wound of the arm – Bristol.
James Thomas, 35, wound of the hand – Bristol.
John Reeves, 31, wound of the head – Bristol.
John Palmon, 32, wound of the hand – Bristol.
Jos. Godfrey, 11, wound of the head – Bristol.
John Jones, 47, wound of the head – Bristol.
Samuel Davis, 31, wound of the head – Westbury, near Bristol.
John Alsop, 50, wound of the head – Bristol.
John Keel, 23, wound of the head – Horfield, near Bristol.
Thomas Hobbs, 24, wound of the wrist – Bristol.
James Bryant, 31, wound of the head – Bristol.
Charles Bishop, 21, wound of the head – Bristol.
Edward Horehound, 29, wound of the head – Bristol.
Cornelius Hickey, 21, wound of the head – St. James's, Bristol.
John Stone, 32, wound of the head – Bristol.

INJURIES IN THE MOB, BUT NOT KNOWN HOW

Thomas Richards, aged 39, wound of the head – Bristol.
Benj. Adams, 38, contused head – Bristol.
George Hanbury, 43, contused face – Bristol.
William Calley, 20, wound of the hip – Bristol.
Michael Carter, 21, wound of the finger – Bristol.
Robert Carpenter, 14, contused face – Bristol.
Daniel Hackett, 12, wound of the face – Bristol.
John Hurley, 21, contused face – Bristol.
William Somers, 13, contused eye – Bristol.
James McKellow, 40, contused shoulder – Bristol.
John Bird, 38, contused arm – Bristol.
Ann Holloway, 21, wound of the eye by a glass bottle – Bristol.
John Williams, 21, apoplexy from intoxication – Bath.
Esau Hunt, 16, apoplexy from intoxication – Bristol.

Only three were brought to the infirmary from excessive drinking, of whom one died. No shot wound amongst the out-casualties. Some of the above were probably sabre wounds. Total of out-casualties, 31. Total number of persons connected with the riots, received at the infirmary, 67, of whom 36 were made in-patients, and 40 known to have been wounded by the military, besides doubtful cases.

IN-CASUALTIES - SHOT WOUNDS

Stephen Bush, aged 20, shot through the chest, died almost immediately – Bristol.
Edward Evans, 17, shot through the right side of the neck near the collar bone, which was fractured by the ball – Bristol.
John Lewis, 30, seaman, shot through the forearm – Bristol.
William Young, 12, shot through the leg – Bristol.
James Salmon, 17, shot in the leg, and one of the bones fractured – Bristol.
John Bennett, 17, shot through the leg – Bristol.
Henry Withers, 20, shot through the leg – Stapleton, near Bristol.
Henry Tuckfield, 17. 17, shot through the thigh – Bristol.
William Clarke, 18, shot through the leg – Clifton.

Thomas Morris, 13, shot through the bowels; since dead – Bristol.

SABRE WOUNDS AND CONTUSIONS FROM THE HORSES OF THE MILITARY

Robert Thompson, aged 60, wounded across the face, which nearly detached the front of his nose – Bristol.
David James, aged 45, wounded across the front of the head, dividing the skull, and penetrating the brain; since dead – Bristol.
James Clarke, aged 34, wound of the head, and contused arm – Bristol.
George Clewell, aged 33, wound of the shoulder and finger – Bristol.
Samuel Vains, aged 16, wound of the head, dividing skull – Bristol.
John Jones, aged 26, wound of the head – Westbury.
Denis Griffiths, aged 30, wound of the head – Bristol.
Abraham Gauntlett, aged 16, compound fracture of the leg – near Bristol.
John Pellowe, aged 17, wound of the head and contusions – Bristol.
William Wilkinson, aged 22, wound of the face and contusions – Bristol.
Michael McCarthy, 35, wound of the head and contusions – Bristol.
John Laurie, 18, wound of the head – Bristol.
Charles Manning, 11, wound of the head – Bristol.
George Parker, aged 25, wound of the head – Horfield, near Bristol.
Charles Stagg, aged 60, wound of the head and contusions – Bristol

ACCIDENTS IN THE MOB AT THE SQUARE AND ELSEWHERE, UNCONNECTED WITH THE MILITARY

John Kelly, aged 19, sprained ankle, in jumping from the window of one of the burning houses – Bristol.
Richard Richards, aged 18, fractured patella, wound of the head and general contusions (occasioned in the same manner) – Horfield.
Charles Bennett, aged 20, compound fractured leg, fractured ankle

and foot, wound of the head, and contusions (occasioned in the same manner) – Bristol.
David O'Donoghue, aged 30, wound of the leg (occasioned by falling through a sash-window) – Bristol.
Mary Cummings, aged 20, burnt in one of the houses which she had entered to plunder (since dead) – Bristol.
William Protheroe, aged 44, burnt and bruised by an accidental fall in the execution of his duty as fireman – Bristol.
Thomas Russell, aged 25, head cut and bruised – Bristol.
Mr Wilcox, aged 34, face cut and bruised by a glass bottle flung at him whilst defending some property – Bristol.
John Connerly, 32, contused head by the staves of the constables – Bristol.
John Southcombe, 21, wound of the bead, and contused shoulder – Bristol.
George Waller Tregallan, 24, apoplexy from drunkenness, since dead – basket-maker at Cathay, Bristol.

Total; 36 – of whom five are dead – namely, two shot, one sabre wound, one excess of drinking, and one burnt. The others are doing well, though some of them are seriously injured, and attended with considerable prospective risk to life and limb. The shot wounds, with one exception, occurred on Sunday morning.

A letter was also published in the *London Packet and New Lloyd's Evening Post* on the same day, in which a visiting inspector reported on the aftermath of the previous week's events for the benefit of its London readership. It provides a unique and detailed glimpse at the recovering city.

'Bristol, Nov. 8.

Dear Sirs,
The town has become so tranquil, that the greater part of the special constables – many of whom did not take off their clothes during the whole of last week - have been dismissed; the great number of military in the place are now affording sufficient protection to the inhabitants against the recurrence

of any outrages. Such was the effect of the liquor taken from the cellars of some of the merchants in Queen Square, by the rioters, that numbers of the savages, after plundering, fell into the Kennet canal and actually lay there insensible while the water flowed over them.

A great deal of property was saved by the Lodgers, in their different houses in Queen Square. In one house, a Mrs Lawrence, from London, had a quantity of plate, jewellery, and diamonds, in the house of a Mrs Busiquet, 49, Queen Square, which she saved, except for some articles, valued between £30. and £40. The deeds of the lady's property, which is valued at nearly one million pounds, were destroyed in the nearby house of her attorney.

We yesterday paid a visit to the New Prison, and found workmen already busily employed in removing the rubbish from the ruins of the governor's house and the chapel, repairing the locks, and laying down the new floors in the debtors' room. The commitments of new prisoners were then going on, and the officials having recovered their confidence, had also resumed their customary importance. About 200 of the rioters have been captured, and about forty of the prisoners, who were liberated, have either been re-taken or have surrendered themselves. The whole are still guarded by soldiers. Upon a careful scrutiny of the personal appearance of all the wretched beings implicated in this unhappy affair, we could discover no faces familiar to our public streets. Two or three of the rioters were identified by a gentleman while we were present; and one in particular, we believe the man who was engaged in setting fire to Mr Lewis's house, was recognised by a person who was endeavouring to rescue the property from the flames. We hear, also, that a man, who came to the infirmary, on Friday, with a severe sabre wound on the head, is recognised as one of those who set fire to the Custom House. He acknowledged having received the wound at that place, but says that he went to look for his brother, who was there burned to death. We have heard that a man is in custody and sworn to as being the person who set fire to Mr Buckley's house, in Queen Square.

The prisoners are of all ages, from 16 to 60; and are, with one or two exceptions, of that class of whom it has been pathetically said, "they rise in the morning without knowing where they shall find food for the day, or rest for the succeeding night." During the short time that could be spared for our examination, we were curious to read the feelings of the prisoners in their countenances, as we passed from cell to cell, and from criminal to criminal. One man we could not help particularising: the mixture of anxiety and ferocity blended in his countenance, gave a most revolting expression to his looks, and the dogged resolution, which came forward at the summons of the turnkey, was particularly disgusting. A few faces looked sorrowful - a larger proportion seemed lost in anxious anticipation of the consequences - some, with a strange anomaly, were careless and laughing; but the greater proportion of the number appeared to be lost in an apathetical indifference to all that was passing around them.

The prisoners are for the present conveyed as usual to the New Prison, two wings of which are still uninjured. However, it is said that it is intended to moor a frigate as near to the prison as is possible, for the reception of all those who shall be found guilty at the next gaol delivery.

I am, yours, faithfully, etc'

Trials of the worst offenders among the rioters were held quickly. By the end of January 1832, no fewer than 102 people had faced trial. Thirty-one were sentenced to death. One man, Christopher Davis, 'a retired tradesman of good circumstances', was sentenced to be hanged merely for shouting a few drunken words of encouragement to the rioters. His harsh sentence was justified because 'the effect of such a man going among a mob must be most mischievous and tends to hold out encouragement to the most depraved portion of society.'

However, after a petition of 10,000 signatures was presented, protesting against the harshness of the death sentences imposed, reprieves were granted to all but four of thirty-one sentenced to death. Remarkably, those signing the petition included many individuals whose homes had been destroyed in the riot.

Eventually, twenty-two people were transported to Australia and the remainder imprisoned.

A third version of the Reform Bill, known as the *Great Reform Act* or the *Representation of the People Act 1832,* was finally placed before Parliament in May 1832. Again, another attempt to block the passage of the *Act* was undertaken by Tory peers in the House of Lords. This led to another period of significant social unrest throughout Britain, known as the 'Days of May.' Thanks partly to public pressure and partly due to the establishment's fear of a French style revolution, the *Great Reform Act* achieved Royal assent in June. The new statute reapportioned constituencies to tackle the unequal distribution of parliamentary seats and extended the franchise among working men and some leaseholders. Voter registration was introduced, and 130 new seats were created in England and Wales.

As a result of the changes, Charles Wetherell lost his

seat in the House of Commons when his 'rotten borough' constituency of Boroughbridge was abolished. He did not sit in Parliament again and passed away in 1846.

The memory of the riots in Bristol, which lived long in the memory of the population, where captured by the artist William James Müller, a witness to the rioting, who produced a remarkably vivid collection of paintings which remain the property of Bristol Museum and Art Gallery to this day.

THE HIDDEN COST OF WAR (PART ONE)

Bristol suffered many casualties during the Second World War. As well as the huge losses suffered by the many regiments of the 'Glosters', the population of the city itself suffered disproportionately during the 'Bristol Blitz', due to its strategic importance in Britain's war effort. 1,300 civilians lost their lives during the air raids that saw the city pounded by the might of the Luftwaffe.

Yet, even a year after the end of hostilities, the war's legacy lingered on in a host of personal and private tragedies hidden among the rows of terraced streets throughout the city. This is one such story.

Despite the first anniversary celebrations in June 1946, marking a year of peace in Europe, the daily drudgery of life felt little like a victory to many. Bread rationing was introduced for the first time, with a promise it would only be for twelve months (it actually lasted for two years), the Communist Party of Great Britain organised sit-ins to demonstrate against the travesty of homelessness when so many buildings sat empty, and housewives spent many hours queuing in the incessant summer rain for ever-dwindling supplies. Meanwhile, many returning soldiers found the adjustment to civilian and family life a difficult one.

In March 1936 , a twenty-one-year-old lorry drivers' mate, Reginald John Frederick Burt (known as 'Jack' to his friends), from Southmead, had married Lily Harris from St Paul's.

Lily was three years younger, aged just eighteen. In 1938 she gave birth to a daughter whom the couple named Barbara. They took a lodging together in Carisbrooke Road. Jack and Lily appeared to be outwardly happy. He found better paid work at the docks, and managed to secure 'easy credit terms' to enable him to furnish their new home.

However, everything was to change on 1st September 1939, when Britain declared war on Germany. Jack was called up in October 1940 and joined the Royal Artillery. It would not be long before he received his first posting and was stationed overseas. With the exception of a short period of compassionate leave in December 1941, Jack Burt would be abroad for more than five years, serving in North Africa, Greece, and Crete. The chances to communicate with home were few and far between.

During her husband's long absence Lily 'formed an attachment' (as it was deftly phrased in the *Western Daily Press*) to an Irish fitter's mate named Thomas O'Connell. She moved out of their home in Carisbrooke Road, into Milsom Street, where the neighbours were unaware of her marital status. On 12th August 1945 Lily gave birth to a son, whom the same newspaper later tactfully informed its readers 'had been born as a result of that association.' Although the war in Europe was now over, Jack Burt remained overseas awaiting his demobilisation papers, and a chance to return to his wife.

On 3rd September 1945, while still stationed in Greece, Jack received the following letter from Lily:

> Dear Jack,
>
> I have no rights to call you husband ever again, and I know what I am going to tell you will shock you, Jack. I had a son a few days ago by another man. I am leaving Milsom Street and moving in with my sister.
> Lil

The bluntness of the communication must have been devastating to the homesick soldier, although his response to Lily seemed a measured one. Burt immediately wrote back, offering to 'take you back my dearest Lil and adopt the child.' He also continued to support her by allowing part of his army pay to be sent to her. His wife must have seriously considered his offer, at least for a short while, as a series of letters then passed between the couple. Eventually, however, Lily decided not to attempt a reconciliation after all, and a few weeks later moved in with her sister Irene at 22 Orange Street in St Paul's. A month or so later, Jack Burt wrote to his mother in Coleford Road, Southmead,

R.A. (Postal Section)
Salonika, Greece
Sept. 30. 1946

Dear Dad and Ma,

Just a few lines hoping you are in the best of health. I have just received a letter from Lil. Ma, I don't know how to tell you. Lil has had a baby boy by another man. Now for God's sake don't go down there and start any trouble. It has broken my heart. All these months she's been writing lovely letters to me, and we were planning what we were going to do when we got a home together. Now she says she has changed her mind and has gone to Irene's. I will go and see her when I return. I can't do anything until I get home … I don't care whatever she has done, I think the world of her.

Your loving son,
Jack

Jack was finally demobbed in May 1946 and returned to Bristol. He was dehydrated, exhausted, and was almost certainly suffering from (undiagnosed) depression. After a few days' recovery in Bristol Royal Infirmary, he was released on Friday 24th May and immediately vowed to visit his estranged wife at her sister's lodgings in St Paul's. Lily's baby son was now nine months old.

It was early evening by the time Jack arrived in Orange Street. His estranged wife and sister-in-law had already left to visit one of the nearby public houses. He knocked on the door but there was no answer (the children had been left with a neighbour). At the very moment Jack knocked on the front door, Lily and Irene had just disappeared out of sight, along Lemon Lane. Had Jack been a few moments earlier – and not stopped for some 'Dutch courage' along the way – perhaps the tragic events of later that evening might have been avoided.

Irene and Lily were met in the pub by Thomas O'Connell, the father of Lily's son. Knowing that her husband was due to call later that night, after being released from hospital, Lily told O'Connell not to accompany them back to Orange Street. 'I need to have things out with Jack,' she told him. The two women left the pub, collected the children, and returned to number 22 Orange Street around 10pm. The street was empty. Meanwhile O'Connell had walked to a nearby fish and chip shop. However, within a few minutes he was knocking loudly on the door at number 22. Lily answered the door, looked nervously left and right along the narrow road of three-storey terraced houses, before ushering her lover in, then sliding the bolt on the inside of the door.

Within moments there was another loud rap on the door. Jack had returned, after his earlier attempt to visit had failed.

He banged loudly on the door and shouted from the street, 'It's me, Jack, I want to see Barbara. Can I see my daughter?'

Lily did not wish to see her husband and remained, silent and unmoving, in the front room. When it seemed that Jack had gone, she tiptoed quickly to the back room, dimming the gaslights as she did so. However, her husband had lingered outside and must have noticed the lights dimming. He impatiently thumped the door again. Lily whispered to her sister, begging her to put the children to bed and to answer the door.

There was another knock on the door, louder still. Jack crouched down and pleaded through the letterbox, 'Lil, let me see my daughter!'

Meanwhile Thomas O'Connell was hastily pushed out of the back door into the yard and told to go home, to make sure he wasn't seen by Jack.

Lily's sister took a moment to calm herself and walked back along the shadowy passage and slid the bolt back, before opening the front door.

'Irene, can I see Lil? I just want to see her and talk to my daughter.'

'Have you had a drink?'

'Yes, but I won't cause no trouble. I love her.'

Irene, probably against her better judgement, let Jack into the house, saying, 'You will have to behave yourself; the flat is rented in my name and I don't want any trouble.'

Jack agreed and picked up his sleepy daughter before carrying her into the room where his estranged wife slept. Irene warned him not to upset Lily.

'You had better not be drunk, Jack! Just leave Lil alone. She's with someone else now.'

Jack ignored her plea, simply saying 'I just want her to come back and live with me again.'

Now regretting her decision to allow Jack in, Irene went into the front room where she slept and closed the door.

In the dimly gaslit back room, Jack placed his daughter onto her small bed and watched while she dozed to sleep. Along the narrow passageway in the front room, Irene lay on her bed, half listening, expecting to overhear an argument erupt between her sister and brother-in-law. Suddenly, as she drifted into a fitful sleep, Irene was awoken with a jolt by an agonising scream that pierced the walls of the house. She sat bolt upright, her heart pounding, as her mind drifted back to consciousness. Footsteps sounded in the passage outside her door. Throwing on her dressing gown, Irene rushed into the passage. The door to Lily's room was open. Through the open doorway, by the light of the flickering gas flame, Irene could see eight-year-old Barbara standing by the fireplace and the baby in its crib. Irene's sister lay prostrate on the bed. Lily's bedsheet, pillow and blankets were stained a crimson red, and her throat had clearly been savagely cut. A thick ribbon of blood had already covered her neck, throat and the upper part of her clothing.

As Irene stepped forward to aid Lily, who was still breathing and seemed to be trying to address her sister, Irene was greeted by the sight of Jack Burt, not in the bedroom, but in the passageway outside the bedroom door. He was returning from the kitchen at the rear of the property, carrying a cup of water. His face was white, and he appeared to be both drunk and traumatised.

'Irene, for God's sake get a doctor. I have cut her throat. I didn't mean to.'

'Oh my God, what have you done?'

'I didn't do it. It was you; you were a bad influence on her! She's my wife.'

Irene lent forward, placing her right ear close to her sister's mouth, while Lily whispered faintly to her. Irene then ran from house, leaving the children in the room next to

their mother's body. It was now midnight. She did not call a doctor, however, but returned with two policeman. She had encountered Sergeant Fisher on St Paul's Street, who in turn contacted Inspector Drinnon, and the two men returned to Orange Street with Irene at 12.50am. Inspector Drinnon entered the back room of number 22 first. He would later record:

'As I entered the room, I saw the accused man sitting on the bed with his head in his hands and crying. He looked up and said: "What have I done? I love my wife." He appeared to have been drinking considerably. His breath smelt of intoxicating liquor but I did not consider him to be drunk. I saw the body of a woman lying on the bed. She appeared to be dead. There was a clasp knife on the bed beside the victim.'

Dr Frederick Jenkins, Bristol Constabulary's deputy police surgeon, was summoned to the crime scene, while Jack Burt was taken to the Central Police Station. Irene was left to comfort the children.

Less than eleven hours after the body of Lily Burt had been discovered, Burt was brought before the bench at Bristol Magistrates' Court in Bridewell Street. Having been stripped of his clothing (which had been removed for forensic examination), Burt was presented in the dock, unshaven, wearing only a pair of police trousers, which were several sizes too large for him, and a grey prison blanket wrapped around him. The accused man held the blanket around himself with one hand and kept his trousers up with the other. When charged with his wife's murder, he was then asked to respond. Burt, appearing to be in a highly distressed condition, murmured only,

'I have nothing to say – nothing to say.'

Superintendent Carter of Bristol C.I.D. successfully applied for Burt to be kept on remand, a free legal aid certificate was granted, and a trial date was set for Monday 1st July 1946 at the Guildhall in Small Street. Jack Burt was not the only person on trial that day. In Germany, Hermann Göring also stood in the dock, facing prosecutors at the Nuremberg war crimes trials.

Jack Burt presented a more sympathetic figure than he had done at his initial hearing, as he appeared shaven, and wearing a dark blue suit, in front of the judge, Mr Justice Morris. When charged with his wife's murder, Burt replied, 'Not guilty.'

Mr Fox-Andrews K.C. appeared for the Crown and Jack Burt was defended by Norman Skelhorn K.C. Unusually, the prosecution began their case with the evidence from three doctors. First to be called was Dr Frederick Jenkins, the deputy police surgeon, who testified,

'When I visited the room at 22 Orange Street it was approximately two hours after the estimated time of death. I saw no evidence of a struggle. I am told that the victim lived for a short while before succumbing to her injuries and was able to speak briefly to her sister.'

'And what was the cause of death, doctor?'

'The victim died from a stab wound to the left side of her neck, causing a severe loss of blood. There was an open clasp knife in the room.'

Dr Jenkins was then shown a small clasp knife, which belonged to the accused man, and had been recovered at the murder scene.

'Dr Jenkins,' Mr Fox-Andrews began, 'This small clasp knife is of the kind of pocketknife commonly issued to serviceman. Do you think it might have caused the death of the victim?'

The doctor nodded, 'Yes, it is certainly capable of having caused the death of this woman. However, if the wound sustained by the victim had been half an inch to either side, it would have missed the jugular vein and might not have been fatal.'

'Thank you, Doctor. Can you add anything else at this stage?'

'Yes, the deceased was four months pregnant.'

There was a murmur of faint disapproval around the public gallery as Dr Jenkins was replaced in the witness stand by Dr Arthur Taylor.

'Dr Taylor, when did you first observe the accused man?'

'I first saw him in the early hours of May 25th, approximately three hours after the victim's presumed time of death. I immediately formed the opinion that the accused man had been taking alcohol and was considerably under the influence of drink. He did not seem to know his wife was dead.'

'Thank you, Doctor.'

Mr Fox-Andrews then called Dr P.W. Parks to the stand, 'Dr Parks, please explain to the court your involvement with the prisoner.'

'Certainly. I am currently the medical officer at Horfield Prison, to where the prisoner was remanded. He was first referred to me about forty-eight hours after his admission to jail. He was then very depressed, extremely distressed, and appeared to be in a kind of dreamlike state. He was very apprehensive and was unable to remember anything about his visit to his wife's house. He was off his food and complained of severe headaches. In my opinion his inability to remember things was not assumed, but genuine.'

'Thank you, Doctor. We now call Irene Harris.'

Lily's sister took the witness stand and was asked to describe the events of 24th May. Clearly upset, she was given a moment to compose herself before Mr Skelhorn was allowed to cross-examine on behalf of the defence.

'Miss Harris, what was the accused man's opinion of you?'

'Sir, he had the idea that I was a bad influence on his wife. He did not like me.'

'And what was your opinion of him? Do you dislike him, do you hate the sight of him?'

'Yes, sir.'

'Miss Harris, did you actually witness my client stab your sister?'

'No, sir. Before she died my sister told me he cut her throat, it wasn't him who told me.'

'You said to the police that he was "fighting drunk", Miss Harris?'

'Yes, sir. I got the impression he did not know what he was doing because he was so drunk.'

'Very well, Miss Harris. Might not your sister have inflicted these wounds upon herself, perhaps in a fit of guilt, or not wishing to have another baby? After all, we only now have your word that it was my client who caused your sister's injuries. And, by your own admission and words "you hate the sight of him".'

'No sir, he did it alright.'

'Very well, no further questions.'

With Mr Skelhorn's cross-examination over, the prosecution called their next witness, Thomas O'Connell, the father of Lily's second child. He received several looks of blatant disapproval from the public gallery as he entered the witness stand. With the war still fresh in the memory, men who had not joined up, and instead appeared to have enjoyed 'a good war', by either profiteering, or taking advantage of absent soldiers' lonely wives and sweethearts, were viewed with almost as much contempt as the accused man in the dock.

'Mr O'Connell, please explain for the court, your involvement in this sad affair.'

'Yes, sir. I am a fitter's mate. I live in Ashley Road and I first met Mrs Burt about eighteen months ago. I visited her at her home.'

'You knew she was a married woman?' Mr Fox-Andrew enquired.

'Yes, sir.'

'You knew her husband was in the army.'

'Yes, sir.'

'You knew he was overseas.'

'Yes, sir. Although, I have seen him on one occasion, but we were not introduced, and there was no trouble.'

In cross-examination Mr Skelhorn, for the defence, asked Thomas O'Connell, 'You slipped out of one door because you thought her husband was coming in another?'

'Quite right, sir. I heard him come in as I was leaving. I didn't want no trouble, you see.'

'Mr O'Connell, were you not away in the armed services during the war?'

'No, sir.'

'And I understand you are a married man?'

'Yes, I am.'

There was another audible murmur of disapproval in the courtroom.

After Thomas O'Connell left the stand, the prosecution concluded their case. The following day would see the defence team present their argument, as they attempted to avoid the hangman's noose for their client, a man who had supposedly murdered his wife and her unborn child.

THE HIDDEN COST OF WAR (PART TWO)

The sun rose on day two of the trial. Jack Burt was ushered into the dock as his defence barrister busied himself, preparing for the vital day ahead. The facts in the case were as brutal as they were polarising. Was the defendant guilty of murder? The appearance on the previous day of the unsympathetic – if not arrogant – Thomas O'Connell in court had perhaps offered the defence a chink of light in the case. Could Norman Skelhorn K.C. take full advantage?

His opening gambit was a risky one, choosing to make a dramatic plea directly to the jury, an address which lasted for one hour and twenty minutes.

'Members of the jury, the defendant who stands before you today served in the army for five years and overseas for three-and-a-half of those. While he was abroad his wife wrote to him, telling him she had had a child by another man. In spite of that, Mr Burt continued his wife's allowance and offered to take her back and adopt the child.'

'This man,' Mr Skelhorn pointed at his client, with a dramatic flourish, 'This man, was serving his country for more than three years abroad, many thousands of miles away. Then one fateful day in September 1945, this letter came to him.'

The letter from Lily to his husband was once again shown to the jury, before Mr Skelhorn continued his passionate address, 'That letter must have arrived with Mr Burt like the explosion of a bomb, and its effect acting just like that of a bombshell – and I use the word "bombshell" in a city I know has suffered its own share of devastating blows during these past few years. The whole of his world must have been broken into bits. Yet, what did he do? Did he immediately seek the most dreadful revenge, as any man might if pushed to the limit? No. Instead, he wrote a most tearful letter to his mother, pleading with her. That was a remarkable letter; there was not one word of recrimination or of desire for revenge. Was this the type of man who would deliberately intend to murder his wife? There are other possible explanations for this tragedy, but surely, it is not a case of murder?'

After his long, impassioned appeal, Norman Skelhorn called Jack Burt's father as his first witness for the defence. John Burt was then asked by the barrister, to testify to his son's relationship with Lily.

'Mr Burt, please identify yourself for the court.'

'I am John Frederick Burt of 15 Coleford Road, Southmead. My son had been happy with his wife, and would never let anyone say a word against her. He once said to me, "I don't care, whatever she's done, I think the world of her." When I visited him in prison he was sat on the bed crying. "I love my wife", he told me.'

The defence counsel then called the defendant himself to answer questions. The spectators in the public gallery leaned forward in hushed anticipation. Always a strategy fraught with risk, defence barristers often choose not to place their clients in the witness box. The possible scenarios could not always be legislated for. Conceivably, the jury might find John Burt an unsympathetic character, making them more, not less, likely to convict him. There was also the distinct possibility that a defendant may fold under a well-constructed cross-examination by the Crown. Perhaps, his answers might appear unconvincing or guarded; leading a jury to believe he was being less than truthful. Only time would tell.

'Mr Burt, when were you and your wife married?'

'In 1936, sir. Then I was called up in October 1940.'

'Up to that time had your married life been happy?'

'Yes, sir.'

'Were you in love with your wife?'

'Very much.'

'And your child, Barbara?'

'Yes, very much.'

'And in 1940 you went into the Forces and in 1942 you went abroad?'

'Yes.'

'Thank you, Mr Burt. Members of the jury, in September 1945 my client received a letter from his wife telling him that she had a baby two days' old and had, and I quote her words, "no right to call you husband ever again." In fact, his wife even sold or gave away all their furniture before moving in with her sister.

My client was serving in Greece, but returned for a short period in October 1945 on compassionate leave. He hoped to save his marriage; offering to help his wife by adopting the illegitimate child, if she agreed to return to him. But she could not make up her mind. He then returned to Greece.

After my client was demobilised in April 1946, he went to live with his mother and father in Coleman Street. He wished his wife to leave Orange Street, and was still willing to have her back. What else could he have done; any reasonable person might ask?'

In allowing Jack Burt to testify in his own defence, Norman Skelhorn had, of course, offered the prosecution barrister the opportunity to question his witness. Would the decision backfire?

Sensing that the jury may have softened towards the defendant, the prosecution immediately adopted an aggressive stance in his cross-examination.

'Mr Burt,' Mr Fox-Andrews began, 'please describe to the court the events of that night.'

'Sir, I do not remember what happened that evening.'

'You do not remember?' Mr Fox-Andrews enquired incredulously, with more than a hint of sarcasm in his voice.

'No, sir. Not really. I have a hazy recollection of going to the house, and all that I can remember after that, is what happened later, at the police station.'

'Really, Mr Burt? That is extremely interesting, since, according to your previous statements, you have never said to the police before that your recollection was hazy.'

'No, sir.'

'Have you made any special effort to remember these things, then, especially for your trial?'

'Yes, sir.'

'Objection, my Lord!' interjected Norman Skelhorn, 'My client has already explained that his recollection of events is hazy.'

'Overruled. The question is a valid one. Please continue Mr Fox-Andrews.'

'Thank you, your honour.' Mr Fox-Andrews took up the reins once again, 'Have you got a bad memory, Mr Burt?'

'No, sir.'

'Good, then perhaps you can remember having been seen by two doctors and two police officers, at various times that night?'

'I have heard it said in court, but I don't remember, sir.'

Mr Fox-Andrews changed his line of attack, as his cross-examination continued, 'On another matter, Mr Burt, why did you also want to see Thomas O'Connell, the Irishman?'

'To tell him to keep away from my wife, sir.'

'Then why could you not have simply taken your wife away from him?'

'Because she was under the influence of Irene Harris.'

'Her sister?'

'Yes, sir.'

'So, Mr Burt, I put it to you that you went to see the Irishman, and you were getting madder all the time?'

'Not madder, sir. Depressed.'

'And you killed your wife?'

'So they tell me.'

'And all you tell us, is that you can't remember?'

'Yes, sir.'

'Yet you remember – in detail – the letter from your wife, the precise date of your demobilisation from the army, and even going to see the Irishman that night?'

'Yes, sir.'

'Very well. No further questions.'

Mr Fox-Andrews sat down, his cross-examination complete, having seemingly dealt a knockout blow to the defence's case.

With that, the defence rested, and Mr Justice Morris instructed both barristers to present their final address to the jury.

Mr Fox-Andrews summed up the prosecution's case succinctly:

'Members of the jury, you have as complete a picture as possible of this tragic affair, and we have established beyond reasonable doubt that this woman was killed by a knife, at the hands of her husband. That, in my opinion, is conclusive. The next step is to consider whether the hand that held the knife struck her voluntarily or not. Whether or not the husband, in fact, knew what he was doing. That, in broad non-legal language, is the main point of the case.

You must decide on that fact. Did he, or did he not, know what he was doing on that night? Although Burt had been drinking all that week, he was still able to go about and do all the things which a normal man is capable of doing. Burt knew that his wife preferred the Irishman, and that she was unwilling to return to him.

I submit, ladies and gentlemen of the jury, that he knew, that when he killed her, he was aware of what he was doing and that he intended to murder her.'

It was now the turn of the defence to make one final plea for mercy before Mr Justice Morris issued his final summation to the jury.

With not much to add to his earlier passionate plea for understanding, Norman Skelhorn could offer little more than a reminder to the jury of Burt's brave service overseas, and his sacrifice on behalf of his country. Would it be enough to sway the jury towards leniency in the case?

Before the jury could make their final deliberations, Mr Justice Morris issued a summation lasting no less than ninety minutes.

'Members of the jury, this has been an unhappy and distressing tragedy. It is not, of course, suggested that the accused man was justified in taking any action against his wife which would lead to her death. The conduct of an erring or unfaithful wife does not justify unlawful or violent conduct on the part of the husband. As far as the case is concerned,' he continued, 'the elements you have to consider in regard to the charge of murder are these – murder will have been committed if someone of sane mind has unlawfully killed another person, with malice and forethought, either expressed or implied.

It has not been suggested to you, members of the jury, that

the accused is anything other than a sane man. However, it has been put to you by the defence, that the defendant was in such a poor physical condition as a result of alcoholic excess, that he was not capable of forming the intention either to kill or to cause grievous bodily harm.

It has been put to you by the defence that there was a killing, and though the killing was an unlawful one, it was not committed with malice and forethought, and therefore amounts not to murder, but to manslaughter.

Evidence of drunkenness, in relation to the accused's incapability to commit the crime, is irrelevant until there is incapacity to form the intention to commit a particular crime. Drunkenness can never be an excuse for crime, but there may be drunkenness to such an extreme form that a drunken man may be wholly incapable of forming the intent required to commit the crime in the first place.

If you are in doubt as to whether the prosecution has proved the element of intention, it would be your duty to return a verdict of manslaughter, provided, of course, that you are satisfied that it was the accused man who was responsible for his wife's death.

If you believe that this man is not guilty of this crime, then you must return just such a verdict. If, on the other hand, you believe he is guilty, then there are only two possible verdicts open to you – murder or manslaughter. Please retire and consider your verdict.'

However, with the time now approaching 5:20pm, Judge Morris decided to finish proceedings for the day. The trial of The Crown v Reginald John Burt would now extend into a third day. The black cap, to be donned by the judge, should he wish to pronounce a sentence of death, would remain with the Clerk of the Court until the following morning. Jack Burt now faced a long and uncomfortable night in the cells as he awaited his fate.

The morning of Wednesday 3rd May 1946 finally arrived.

With Judge Morris's long and precise definition of the law no doubt still fresh in their minds from the previous day, the jury duly retired to consider their verdict. The packed gallery sat in nervous anticipation. The time was now 10:00am.

Neither the members of the public wedged into every available seat in the gallery, nor the accused man himself, would need to wait for long for the fruits of the jury's deliberations. At 10:15am the twelve members of the jury filed dutifully back to their seats.

'Members of the jury, have you reached a verdict?'

'We have, your honour. We find the prisoner not guilty on the count of murder.'

'And on the count of manslaughter?'

'We find the prisoner guilty of manslaughter.'

Mr Justice Morris would have no need for the black cap. In passing sentence, he told Jack Burt, 'I should not be discharging my public duty if I passed on you any sentence less than five years' penal servitude. Take the prisoner away.'

Following the trial, Superintendent Carter of Bristol C.I.D. revealed to the public that, five years earlier, in December 1941, Burt had been arrested and charged with being, 'drunk and disorderly, assaulting his wife and being drunk while having a four-year-old child in his charge.' He was, at that time, already on probation for another similar offence. No action was deemed necessary at the time, as the offences were felt to be of a relatively minor nature. Perhaps, if more punitive action had been taken in 1941, Lily Burt's life may have been a very different one.

Society's attitude towards drunkenness in serious criminal cases had hardened considerably during the first half of the twentieth century. Throughout the Victorian era it

was entirely conceivable that Jack Burt's twin 'defence' of drunkenness, coupled with his wife's behaviour while he was away serving his country, might have seen him acquitted. However, a substantial effort to reduce the worrying number of alcohol related crimes, together with government concern over the effect of drink on the country's war effort, had seen tolerance towards drunkenness reduced significantly.

Nevertheless, Burt's status as a returning soldier no doubt played in his favour. Coupled with a growing public distaste for capital punishment, the unsympathetic persona of the third point in this tragic love triangle, Thomas O'Connell, undoubtedly helped Burt escape the hangman.

Partly as a result of Jack Burt's trial, and other similar cases, some clearer definitions of mitigating circumstances in cases of unlawful killing were made in the *Homicide Act 1957*. This had the effect of decreasing the number of murder convictions resulting in a sentence of death. However, it would be a further eight years until the death penalty itself was suspended in law (and another thirty-three years until it was finally abolished altogether, in 1998).

Following his release from Horfield Prison in 1949, Jack Burt did not appear to have troubled the police again. He remarried during the 1950s, and eventually passed away in 1978 at the age of sixty-four. Both Jack Burt and Thomas O'Connell stayed in Bristol until their deaths, although both men remained lifelong enemies, each blaming the other for their respective loss.

THE ODEON CINEMA MURDER (PART ONE)

You may remember, in the chapter entitled *The Portway Taxicab Murder*, that in 1947, defence barrister Charles Ingle K.C. had taunted Detective-Superintendent Fred Carter in court, over the police's inability to solve the infamous one-year-old slaying of popular cinema manager Robert Jackson. The newspapers had been quick to label that puzzling case *'The Odeon Cinema Murder'*. But why had the case already achieved such infamy, and are we really any closer now to piecing together the events of Wednesday 29th May 1946?

It is hard now to imagine just how popular the cinema industry was in its heyday during the 1930s and 1940s. Almost everyone in Britain visited their local cinema at least once a week, and many people did so two or three times. In 1946, UK cinema audiences reached an historic high of 1.64 billion attendances, with several screenings a day, and any town or city of an appreciable size boasted a number of busy playhouses. A visit to the 'flicks' was a welcome distraction from the recent horrors of war and the daily drudgery of continuing rationing, at the same time providing the weary population with some affordable entertainment.

However, the immediate postwar period had also seen an alarming rise in violent robberies, especially those involving a firearm. With a substantial quantity of army service weapons still in circulation across the country, combined with the large number of disaffected returning soldiers, this was perhaps

not surprising. Even the movies had begun to reflect the increasingly dark and violent side of human nature. Yet, the drama that unfolded at the Odeon cinema in Bristol, on the early evening of 29th May, took place off-screen instead.

The Odeon cinema, on the junction of Union Street and Broadmead, was the city's largest and most popular cinema in the immediate postwar years. Although it still survives to this day, the Odeon in 1946 was a much grander affair. Today, the fabric of the building is much changed. The cinema now comprises three smaller screens on the upper levels, while the ground level, which once contained an attractive foyer, with marble pillars and a mosaic-tiled floor, now contains a supermarket and clothes store. The Odeon originally comprised of a voluminous single auditorium with floodlit pillars, housing nearly 2,000 green baize seats and deep, luxurious carpets. The ceiling was gilded with painted stars and attractive lighting, and its majestic rotunda entrance tower was floodlit at night and adorned with custom made, black plate glass. Inside, two sweeping staircases led to an upper foyer and balcony which housed a circular lounge, restaurant, and the manager's office. The founder of the Odeon Cinema chain himself, Oscar Deutsch, had officially opened the cinema in 1938, and his wife, Lillian, had personally chosen the decoration and colour scheme.

Nevertheless, the events of Wednesday 29th May were about to cast a dark cloud over the magic of the movies.

That night, a large crowd had queued patiently on a warm early summer's evening, waiting for the 6:25pm screening of *The Light That Failed*, starring Ronald Colman and Ida Lupino. This version of Rudyard Kipling's story about an artist who was losing his eyesight had actually been filmed in 1939, but its release had been delayed until after the war as its content was considered too downbeat and depressing for wartime audiences. Nevertheless, this was no reflection on the film's popularity. By 6:25pm, almost all of the 2,000 seats were filled, as the audience enjoyed a cigarette while watching the pre-film newsreels, together with a trailer for the upcoming movie *The Captive Heart* starring Michael Redgrave. Upstairs at the Odeon cinema that night, scores of others had congregated in the restaurant and lounge area. It would have been an easy enough task for the murderer or murderers to have entered the premises unnoticed.

The timing of the events that followed is crucial and, as well as forming the crux of the initial police investigation, has shaped part of the legend which has grown up around the murder of cinema manager Robert Parrington-Jackson that night.

At approximately 6:35pm the first reel of *The Light That Failed* flickered onto the screen and the audience fell silent. At that same moment, Robert Parrington-Jackson removed the takings from the box office cash desk and took them upstairs to be counted and placed in the office safe. Although the foyer and balcony were now much quieter, there were still several people congregated in the upstairs lounge or sat in the restaurant. Two minutes later, at 6:37pm, the uniformed doorman Charlie Jackson (no relation to the manager) was handed some lost property – a purse – which he took upstairs to deposit in the manager's office. At that time most cinemas employed a uniformed doorman, in a similar fashion to an upmarket hotel, to hold open the door and greet customers with a cheerful 'Good evening'. However, on reaching Mr Parrington-Jackson's office on the balcony level, the doorman found the door shut. At the later inquest he explained what happened next.

'Someone came to me with some lost property, a purse, which they had picked up in the stalls. I took it upstairs intending to give it to Mr Jackson. His door was shut though, and I waited, because I thought he would be checking the money and putting it away, and would not want to be disturbed.'

The staff referred to the manager either as just 'Mr Jackson', rather than his full name, or sometimes simply as 'Jacko'.

The cinema's takings that night amounted to £800 in cash; a substantial sum of money, equating to approximately £30,000 today.

'Shortly after,' the doorman continued, 'Mr Jackson came out and I handed the lost property to him. He returned to the office and I went down to the foyer.' The door to the manager's office was spring-loaded and closed automatically behind Mr Jackson, meaning that the doorman did not have the opportunity to see if anyone else had been inside. It was now 6:40pm.

On returning to the foyer, the doorman heard a bang,

which (according to his later testimony) he instinctively sensed had come from upstairs. It was now 6:42pm. 'I immediately went up to the balcony to make enquiries into the cause of the bang,' he explained. 'I did not go into the office, but walked around the balcony. Shortly after, I went for the police.'

This raises three important questions. Firstly, if the unusual noise the doorman heard had definitely come from upstairs, and he deemed it sufficiently worrying to immediately race to the balcony level to investigate, why did he not check the manager's office, before going to the police station? It would have been instantly obvious that the sound had not emanated from the restaurant or lounge area, as nothing appeared to be out of the ordinary there. Even if he did not wish to disturb Mr Jackson, why not at least knock on the door and check that everything was alright? This leads neatly to the next puzzling conundrum. The doorman, rather than investigating the unusual sound, immediately decided to contact the police. Yet, the staff at the adjacent balcony restaurant must have also heard the noise, but continued to serve customers as normal. Although Mrs Mary Alcock, the restaurant supervisor, had heard the strange bang at the same time, she did nothing other than ask the doorman what had caused it. He told her that he did not know but that 'it was probably just noises from the soundtrack of the film playing downstairs.'

The Light That Failed had been showing three times daily since the previous Thursday and most of the Odeon's staff would have no doubt become accustomed to this. Reassured, Mary Alcock then returned to the counter inside the restaurant. The restaurant manageress, Mrs Metcalf, calling from the kitchen (and who had, presumably, not considered the sound to be anything out of the ordinary), then asked her, 'Mary, will you go and see if Mr Jackson is ready for his tea?'

Mary Alcock explained at the later inquest that, 'I went

and found Mr Jackson's door shut. I knocked and got no answer. I knocked again and then opened the door. I found Mr Jackson lying just inside the door on his right side. He had been wounded in the head, but he did not speak. I then went back to get my manageress, Mrs Metcalf and told her. I assumed that Mr Jackson had attempted to take his own life.'

Based on Mrs Alcock's later testimony, the manager was alone in the office; at least that was her impression. She had no reason to assume otherwise, since no one had been seen entering or exiting. Two shots had been fired. The first had missed Mr Jackson; the bullet having lodged itself in the wall. The second shot had entered the manager's head, three inches above his right eye, causing a fracture of the skull and a cerebral haemorrhage. A spent cartridge lay on the floor close to his prostrate body. Robert Parrington-Jackson was rushed to Bristol Royal Infirmary but sadly never regained consciousness. He died the following morning. His death had now become a murder enquiry.

The very important question of the telephone should also be considered at this point. The only telephone at the Odeon was located in the manager's office. Yet rather than telephone the police from there, the doorman had instead chosen to go downstairs, exit the Odeon, then go on foot along Broadmead, turn right into Silver Steet, then left into Bridewell Street, before arriving at the Bridewell Police Station approximately five minutes later. He then returned on foot to the cinema with two uniformed officers and two detectives. This process took between ten and fifteen minutes, which may have allowed Mr Jackson's killer, or killers, to escape. The 999-emergency telephone service had yet to be introduced to Bristol, despite having been in operation in London since 1937. Was this the reason the doorman chose this more circuitous method of contacting the police, or did he have a deeper motivation?

Detective-Superintendent Fred Carter was immediately placed in charge of the investigation. Two uniformed officers were placed outside the manager's office while detectives began their investigation. Unusually, and perhaps significantly, the 2,000 strong audience in the auditorium were not immediately informed of the tragedy. Did this allow the killer, or killers, to simply return to the auditorium after shooting Mr Jackson, and then hide in plain sight among the other cinemagoers? With the exception of one message, which briefly flashed up on the screen, asking if there was a doctor in the house, the audience was blissfully unaware of the drama taking place in the office upstairs. This immediately raised one very obvious question: why did no one in an audience of almost 2,000 people hear the shots? After all, the doorman, who was also downstairs, heard them. Cinema auditoriums were not routinely soundproofed at that time, and the sound systems were not as advanced (or as loud) as might be expected in a modern movie multiplex. The answer has grown into part of the legend surrounding the story of Robert Jackson's death, and has led some to theorise that his murder was meticulously planned, down to the exact second. The reason for the audience failing to hear the gunshots is a simple one.

There are two scenes during the opening eight minutes of *The Light That Failed*, during which the sound of gunfire can be heard on the screen. Initially, two rounds are fired by the characters on screen, followed by another two rounds, finishing with a single shot. This action takes place one minute and twenty-six seconds into the film, and is completed within twenty-nine seconds. There is a pause of a few seconds between the bursts of gunfire. Many of those who have investigated this case believe that the noise of gunfire on screen masked the sound of two shots being fired simultaneously upstairs in Robert Jackson's office. It must be stressed that, if the shooting had been deliberately planned to coincide with the onscreen noise of gunfire, it would have required extraordinary timing and seems almost impossible to carry out successfully. Besides, as the film began at 6:35pm, this would have placed the shooting between 6:36 and 6:37pm. We know this cannot be the case, as the doorman testified to seeing Mr Jackson come out of his office briefly at 6:40pm, before returning inside. This theory, then, seems unlikely. However, just three and a half minutes later, there is a sustained Sudan battle sequence in *The Light That Failed*, which lasts from five minutes and twenty-five seconds into the picture, and continues for two minutes and thirty seconds. This onscreen battle features repeated gunshots, cavalry charges, loud music, and the general tumult of battle. With the film commencing at 6:35pm, this sequence would have occurred between approximately 6:41pm and 6:44pm, and seems to align itself precisely with the last known sighting of Mr Jackson alive. Not only does this give us an exact time of death; it appears to explain why no one in the auditorium heard the sound of gunshots being simultaneously fired in the upstairs office. Was this extraordinarily detailed planning and execution on the part of the perpetrators, or merely remarkably good fortune? We do not know the answer. However, it raises several interesting questions – some of which will be addressed as the story unfolds.

Meanwhile, Detective-Superintendent Fred Carter begin began his investigation in earnest. The initial conundrum which presented itself, was that of motive. A planned robbery of the cinema's takings seemed the obvious intention. The sum of £800 (which represented the takings from just two screenings that day) would have been a considerable haul, especially as the Odeon cinema had far less security in place than, perhaps, might be expected at a bank or in a factory wages office on payday. During the war years, and immediately afterwards, cinemas were considered 'easy' and lucrative targets for the criminal underworld. Yet, despite the risks taken that night by the thief in entering Mr Jackson's office, the money remained in the safe, the safe locked and untouched, and the keys still in the manager's jacket pocket. Was this significant? Had the thief merely panicked after shooting Robert Jackson, then fled empty-handed? If so, why, since the sound of gunfire had not caused any immediate alarm to be raised? Or had the robber instead remained hidden in the office the entire time? DS Fred Carter weighed up all these intriguing possibilities. If the gunman had methodically and coldheartedly planned the shooting of the manager to coincide precisely with the sound of gunfire during the screening of *The Light That Failed*, as it played simultaneously downstairs, then surely he would not have panicked so easily. This anomaly seemed to discount the possibility that the shooting had been premeditated. This left the police with three probable solutions.

The first possibility was that the manager had taken his own life. However, this option was almost immediately ruled out by detectives. Shortly before being shot, Mr Jackson had been seen laughing and joking with other members of staff. Furthermore, there was no weapon found beside his body, nor anywhere else in the room, and there were no gunpowder residue markings on the victim's face, which seemed to indicate that the shots had been fired from a distance of more than six feet away, and therefore certainly not self-inflicted. This provided the answer to one question; that it was not suicide. But where was the gun and who removed it from the room?

Conceivably, then, the fatality had been an accident after all. Had the thief simply panicked and ran, after inadvertently having discharged their firearm while attempting to coerce Mr Jackson into opening the safe? This was a possibility, although it did raise two further questions: why bring a loaded gun to a crime scene, only to panic after firing it, and then shoot twice? One shot may have been accidental, but surely not two?

One of the bullets fired had missed its intended target altogether, yet the second projectile had entered the victim's skull in what appeared to be an almost execution style murder. Perhaps, then, DS Carter theorised, there was more to the killing of the cinema manager than a simple robbery gone wrong. The police decided to dig a little deeper into Robert Jackson's background.

Robert Nelson Parrington-Jackson was a flamboyant, even glamorous, character. Aged just thirty-three at the time of his death, Jackson had already experienced life to the full. After taking a steamship to New Orleans in 1937, he had driven a racing car across America, ending up in California, where he tried his hand as a radio presenter and actor, apparently even appearing as an extra in the Errol Flynn movie *The Adventures of Robin Hood*. After returning to England, he had briefly taken over as manager of the Odeon in 1939, just prior to the outbreak of war, before volunteering to serve in the Royal Navy. Following his demobilisation from the forces in 1946, Jackson had returned to the cinema just a few weeks before his untimely death, yet he had already made a favourable impression with his superiors; so much so, that a special screening of *The Captive Heart* had been arranged for the following week, with the Lord Mayor of Bristol as a special guest. 'Jacko' always wore a dinner jacket during the evening screenings at the Odeon, and would greet the usherettes, waitresses, and kiosk girls with a friendly hug and kiss. Despite being married with a four-year-old son, Robert

Jackson had developed a reputation for his over familiarity with the female staff at the Odeon. As DS Carter unpeeled each layer of Jackson's past, further revelations presented themselves. One usherette at the Odeon told the authorities that 'he used to think of himself as a real lad.' Instead of being what was termed at the time as 'popular with the ladies', he was, in fact, disliked. Most of the female employees at the time considered him rude, inappropriate, obnoxious, and 'the kind of man who liked to get his own way.' Conceivably, then, there was an entirely different motive behind his shooting. Had an upset employee pulled the trigger? Or perhaps even a jealous boyfriend or husband had sought out a confrontation with the amorous manager, who was abusing his position of authority.

DS Fred Carter had many possibilities to consider as he continued his search for the killer. Firstly, however, as with all suspicious deaths, came the formality of the coroner's inquest.

THE ODEON CINEMA MURDER (PART TWO)

A large and expectant crowd gathered at the inquest as DS Carter described how he and his men had arrived quickly at the Odeon cinema on the night of the shooting.

'We found a .45 bullet cartridge case from an American Colt automatic pistol in the office. There was also a bullet found there which would fit that weapon.'

'And are you carrying out extensive enquiries by every available means?' asked Mr A.E. Baker, the Bristol coroner.

'Yes, sir,' replied DS Carter. 'We have confirmed that no gun was officially kept at the cinema, and after two days and nights of intensive search at the cinema and its precincts, we have been unable to find the weapon, which means it is almost certainly not there. A watch is being maintained at Temple Meads as well as other West Country stations, and at Avonmouth and other docks. All likely places, including blitzed ruins, have been combed for the weapon, but so far without result.'

'And so far, I understand, you have been unable to charge anybody with the occurrence?'

'That is so, sir.'

Next, Professor James M. Webster, the Home Office pathologist, submitted the results of his post-mortem.

'The victim, Mr Robert Nelson Parrington-Jackson, was thirty-three years of age and had been otherwise in good health. There was a firearm wound in the deceased man's head, the entry point being three inches above and to the side of the right eye. The point of exit was by the left eye, traversing the brain and left eye, causing a fracture of the skull, and laceration of the brain, and cerebral haemorrhage. The course of the bullet was from above, and fired downwards, from entering the right side of the victim's skull and exiting to the left. There was no burning on the face, no blackening, and only two particles of burnt powder on the face or clothing.'

'As you might expect to find if it had been a close discharge from the weapon?' clarified the coroner.

'Yes, sir.' replied Professor Webster.

'Was it possible, in your opinion, for him to have inflicted this wound himself, Professor?'

'No, in my opinion, this was not a self-inflicted wound.'

'And the cause of death, Professor?'

'The cause of death was cerebral haemorrhage and fracture of the skull, due to the passage of a bullet and consequent laceration of the brain, due to a firearm shot from a weapon of a heavy calibre.'

At this point the inquest was adjourned to allow the police to proceed with their investigation.

Enquiries among the cinema's staff quickly revealed the presence of two men whose behaviour and appearance had attracted attention that night. Three days after Robert Jackson's murder, DS Carter issued a statement detailing the description of two individuals whom the police wished to question. The first man had been witnessed on the night of the murder eating sardines on toast in the restaurant, around 5:45pm. After finishing, at approximately 6:40pm, he took a seat on one of the settees on the cinema's balcony, adjacent to the manager's office, and thumbed through a newspaper. He was described in the *Western Daily Press* as being,

'Aged twenty-five to twenty-eight, five feet nine or ten

inches high, thin build, dark brown hair, sallow complexion, clean shaven, rather sunken cheeks, decaying teeth, thin or pursed lips, blue eyes, and long thin fingers. He was dressed in a well-worn and untidy navy-blue suit, shiny in places, white shirt, with white soft collar and necktie. He was not wearing a hat, and was carrying an old, soiled mackintosh.'

Members of staff also variously described him as appearing 'rather neglected in appearance', 'shifty', and 'nervous.'

A second man had been spotted by an usherette on the evening prior to the murder (Tuesday 28th May) loitering on the balcony lounge from 5:30pm to just after 6:00pm. The usherette had asked the man if he needed anything, to which he had replied, 'No, I'm just waiting for someone.' Was he genuinely waiting for his sweetheart, or perhaps he was 'casing the joint'? The descriptions of the two men were remarkably similar – particularly the thin or pursed lips – eventually leaving the police to deduce that they were probably looking for one man, rather than two.

Despite the colourful description, little in the way of positive new information resulted. Another witness did contact the police claiming that she had seen a scruffy man in the Odeon's restaurant eating sardines on toast that night, and that there was a second man at his table. However, she was unable to confirm whether the two men had spoken to each other and no one else was able to confirm her sighting. A waitress working in a Clifton café reported serving 'a man with pursed lips' on the day after the murder, but the police were not able to trace him. The 'neglected-looking' man's description was also flashed onto cinema screens around Bristol and Bath for several days, but this yielded little response. Perhaps this man was not local; DS Carter was certainly beginning to think so.

Meanwhile, detectives continued to work diligently on the other puzzling aspects of their investigation. Firstly, since no one had recalled seeing anyone suspicious leaving the office or the cinema building immediately following the shooting. This left three possibilities: either the man had returned to the auditorium and managed to blend into the 2,000 strong crowd, still carrying the weapon used in the murder; that he was still hiding somewhere inside the manager's office or within the building; or, lastly, that he had managed to escape undetected. The first possibility seemed the least likely – 'criminal folly', in the words of DS Fred Carter. Had the man attempted to retake his seat among the audience, he might have risked attracting attention, not to mention requiring nerves of steel to appear unflustered during the police questioning that immediately followed the ending of the screening that night. In addition, since the gun used in the murder was not found anywhere in the cinema, the attacker must have still had the weapon secreted about his person. This seemed a huge risk for anyone to take, when the obvious answer would have been to leave the premises immediately. As the intensive search of the cinema had yielded no weapon, nor anyone in hiding, it was safe to assume that the killer had escaped into the busy city centre on foot. But how had he managed to vanish into thin air?

Another examination of the manager's office quickly provided the answer. At the back of Mr Jackson's office, a small maintenance hatch led into a crawl space, or void, underneath the balcony of the cinema. Unseen from the floor above, or the foyer below, the murderer or murderers would have been able to crawl between the girders and rafters via another hatch and into the passageway leading to the Odeon's gallery exit on Union Street. Right under the noses of 2,000 customers and staff, the killer had got clean away. DS Carter issued another statement to the press, but it was probably already too late.

'To escape that way, the wanted man must be agile and resourceful. If anyone saw a man looking excited or dishevelled, or with dust and cobwebs on his clothes and hands, leaving the cinema by the Union Street gallery exit between 6:45pm and 7:30pm on Wednesday night, he or she should at once communicate with the police. That man may have been the murderer. With luck – and luck obviously favoured him that night – he could have got clean away by that route.'

However, with so many people on the busy city centre streets that night, no one came forward with a potentially decisive lead; the investigation remained stalled.

Next for detectives came the singular type of gun used in the killing, an US Army issue Colt 45 automatic pistol. While this might appear to indicate an American assassin, perhaps an ex-serviceman, this was not necessarily the case. Britain was awash was handguns in the immediate postwar period. Hundreds of thousands of soldiers had returned home, many of them bringing with them souvenir guns from their wartime adventures, or failing to hand back their service weapons, as required by law. As this legislation tightened, many guns found their way onto the black market, into the hands of criminals, or were simply thrown into rivers and lakes. To further complicate matters, the Colt .45 had remained virtually unchanged since its introduction in 1911, meaning the bullet that killed Robert Jackson may have actually been fired from a gun left over from the First World War. In addition, the weapon itself had still to surface. Once again, the investigation hit a brick wall.

At last, what appeared to be a breakthrough for the beleaguered DS Carter and the Bristol C.I.D. finally came on 28th June, over eighty miles away, and in the most tragic of circumstances. The body of a twelve-year-old girl, Muriel Drinkwater, was discovered in woods adjacent to her family home in Penllergaer, near Swansea in South Wales. A forensic examination soon discovered that Muriel had been shot twice. The weapon was unearthed close by, two days later – a World War One Colt .45 pistol. Inspector Benson, from the South Wales Police, immediately informed his colleagues in Bristol C.I.D. as a forensic examination of the weapon was undertaken. Fortuitously, the Colt Manufacturing Company kept a detailed record of all serial numbers, making the tracing of the weapon's history a relatively easy one. The pistol used to murder Muriel Drinkwater, which bore the serial number 1142684 (A1), had been originally manufactured in 1943 for the US Army, and had since been modified with the distinctive addition of a new Perspex handle to replace the original worn out grip. Surely someone would now be able to identify this unique firearm. Yet, despite South Wales police questioning more than 1,500 men locally, and commissioning a detailed forensic examination of the gun, the weapon could not be conclusively matched to the one used in the killing of Robert Jackson at the Odeon cinema. The description of the man seen acting suspiciously in Penllergaer on the day of Muriel's disappearance however, seemed to closely match the man sought by Bristol police:

"Scruffy dark hair, aged about thirty, worn blue suit."

This man was never located, and although other suspects emerged, the murder of Muriel Drinkwater remains unsolved to this day.

Meanwhile in Bristol, as attempts to link the recovered Colt .45 pistol with the Odeon shooting had proved inconclusive, it seemed that DS Carter was back to square one. On 2nd August, a second inquest formally recorded that 'the death, in accordance with the medical evidence, was due to murder by person or persons unknown.' Some disquiet was also expressed at the inquest, regarding the Bristol police's lack of progress in the case. In the weeks that followed, a minor local criminal contacted the *Bristol Post* and the *Western Daily Press*, claiming that police officers were trying to 'fit me up with the cinema murder, unless I cooperate.' It seemed public expectation was weighing heavily on Bristol C.I.D. and Detective-Superintendent Carter personally, who was given two weeks leave.

However, a remarkable discovery by a member of the public at the end of August dramatically changed the course of the investigation. A Colt .45 was handed in to Bristol C.I.D. by a man who had discovered the weapon in a static water tank, approximately half a mile from the murder scene. Many such water tanks had been erected around the city during the blitz of Bristol, to provide water for firefighters. This pistol seemed the most probable murder weapon, as well as providing police with the killer's likely escape route on the night of the murder. Although the gun and bullet could not be conclusively linked, nor any witnesses to its disposal found, the discovery did push the investigation in another direction. What if the killer had been an American soldier after all? Although the war had ended a year earlier, there were still many US servicemen stationed in the southwest; in fact, the American Forces even maintained a prison and execution block at nearby Shepton Mallet, only twenty miles away.

A number of G.I.s were questioned. One, a sergeant in the Marines, was even held in the cells for several days. The Colt .45 was thrown down on the desk in front of him and he was threatened with 'taking the fall' for the Odeon murder unless he confessed. Ultimately, however, each one had a suitable alibi and without any fingerprint evidence from the manager's office at the Odeon, they were all released without charge.

It would not be until November that providence

provided Bristol police with another person of interest in their investigation. Unfortunately for the Bristol C.I.D., the description of the suspect differed wildly from the 'neglected-looking' man seen on the balcony of the Odeon.

US Army deserter Freeman Reese had absconded from an American military camp in Lichfield, after being placed in the 'glasshouse' for the offence of using a 'whites only' toilet. He was believed to have been involved in the robbery of a safe at the Picturedome Cinema in Burton-on-Trent, in the Midlands, during which Police Constable Brindley Booth had been killed. The robbery had taken place less than twenty-four hours before the shooting of Robert Jackson in Bristol. On paper at least, Reece seemed a plausible suspect. Once the description of Reese had been circulated to all police forces in the country, it became abundantly apparent that his description could not have contrasted more with that of the man sought in the Bristol Odeon killing:

'Wanted for murder and robbery. Freeman Reese, a coloured man who is a deserter from the US Army. Aged twenty-six, height six feet one inch, weight about 150lbs, black hair, brown complexion.'

It was yet another red herring for the Bristol C.I.D. and DS Fred Carter.

The story of Freeman Reese caused a public sensation at the time and, in a transparent example of the racism inherent in society during the postwar period, many black G.I.s were hounded by members of the public during the search for the absent soldier, to the point where several were given certificates by their local police force, signed by the Chief-Constable, guaranteeing that they were NOT Freeman Reese.

Reese managed to successfully evade capture for another ten years, until he was arrested on the Isle of Man in 1956. He was cleared of any involvement in PC Booth's murder.

However, as he left court, he was promptly re-arrested and sentenced to twenty years for desertion from the army.

Back in Bristol, the hunt for the Odeon murderer eventually ran out of steam. The best efforts of detectives to trace the owner of the pistol, or the 'neglected-looking' man were all unsuccessful. Occasionally officers received another tantalising clue. Several months after the murder, an anonymous letter arrived at Bridewell Police Station instructing the police to look for, 'a man in his thirties, smartly dressed, with a shirt and tie.' However, with little else to go on, the lead proved to be yet another dead end.

In 1949, the chief clerk of Lloyds Bank in Knowle, Bristol, was shot and killed during a robbery. An anonymous source tipped off the police, telling them that the two cases were linked, and to look for a 'blonde lady'. The course of that investigation and its possible connection to this case is covered in the chapter *Murder on Wells Road.*

As the years passed, the trail for the killer of Robert Parrington-Jackson grew cold, although the notoriorty surrounding the case lingered on; principally the persistent rumour that the cinema manager had been shot by a jealous boyfriend or husband. During the 1970s, a man contacted the *Bristol Post*, but refused to give his name. He told a reporter that:

'Jacko was the sort of bloke who would always greet his usherettes and kiosk girls with a hug or a kiss. I believe it led to one their boyfriends becoming jealous. Something happened to one of the girls in the kiosk and although Jacko had nothing to with it, he apparently got the blame.'

Although the Bristol C.I.D. investigated the claim they never took the jealous lover angle seriously, always believing that robbery had been the intended motive.

Whatever the cause of Mr Jackson's death, a ghostly aspect has now grown around his murder. Screen three of the modern Odeon is now reputed to be one of Bristol's most haunted locations. Staff have reported seeing the ghost of a man wandering around the auditorium, who mysteriously vanishes if approached. One particular seat in the third row is said to be haunted by a shadowy figure who remains seated at the end of the film, only to disappear when he is approached. During the 1990s a clairvoyant was employed on two occasions to exorcise an apparition which allegedly appeared within the walls of the clothes store on the ground floor (which now occupies the original Odeon cinema's foyer).

Finally, many years later, there was a resolution of sorts in the case. In 1989, a petty crook from South Wales apparently admitted to the murder on his death bed. Billy Fisher, known to the underworld as 'The Fish', confessed to his son, Jeff, that in 1946 he had travelled with his accomplice, Dukey Leonard from South Wales, intent on robbing the Odeon. However, the thieves panicked when Robert Jackson unexpectedly walked into the office. He was then shot twice by 'The Fish' before both men hurriedly escaped.

Jeff Fisher agonised over his father's confession for several years, before finally telling the police in 1993, mainly because he believed that his father may have been involved in many more unsolved crimes, even other murders. There certainly does not appear to be any reason for his father to have lied on his death bed. Yet, despite his apparent admission of guilt, without any evidence to directly link Billy Fisher to the murder, nor an opportunity for the police to question him, the case remains officially unsolved.

Despite Billy Fisher's confession, many questions remain unanswered. Was the Odeon cinema murder linked to other unsolved crimes? How did the killer, or killers, make their getaway so easily? How could they have possibly known about the existence of the narrow crawlspace between the girders under the balcony? Perhaps they received a 'tip-off' or inside help? And, what of the cinema doorman's inexplicable behaviour on the night of the murder? Was he the 'smartly dressed man in his thirties', that the anonymous caller to the *Bristol Post* hinted at?

Even with forensic advances such as DNA, the murder of Robert Parrington-Jackson is still officially unsolved, despite a further cold case review in 2006. We will probably never know what really happened in the manager's office on the night of 29th May 1946.

It remains the oldest cold case on the files of Avon and Somerset Police.

MARKET FORCES – THE OLD MARKET RIOTS

A century after the Bristol Riots of 1831, another set of circumstances would once again lead the city into revolt. This time the catalyst would not be the fundamental right to vote; on this occasion the spark that would ignite the flame came from the denial of another basic need, the right to work and to feed your family.

The seeds of the Bristol Riots of 1932 had already been sown a decade or more earlier, when a million British soldiers returned from the Great War. A year later, a third of these men were still unemployed. By 1921, total unemployment in Britain had soared to more than 2.5 million. It stayed well above one million for almost all the interwar period. Following the stock market crash in 1929, the queue at the country's labour exchanges contained more than three million people: one in five of all British workers.

Bristol was particularly badly affected. By 1920 it was estimated there were at least 7,000 unemployed men in the city, of which at least 6,000 were returning servicemen. Many suffered from mental health issues relating to their combat experiences in the trenches. Poverty, poor housing and unsanitary conditions, coupled with a city-wide rat infestation, only exacerbated the problem.

In 1919 the *Rats and Mice Destruction Act* was passed, obliging all householders to destroy any rats or mice which might be nesting on their property. During 'National Rat

Week' in February 1920 (the third such week in less than a year), Bristol householders laid down 263,000 poison rat baits and the Corporation set down 5,300 traps of their own around the city.

The 1920s saw a series of strikes and protests across the city, notably during the General Strike of 1926 when 18,000 Bristol workers downed tools. A week later the number had doubled. Yet, none of these rallies tipped over into the violence witnessed during what became known as the Old Market Riots. So, what factors pivoted the city's workers to swing from peaceful demonstration to riot and destruction in 1932?

By the beginning of 1931 unemployment in Britian had peaked. Numerous Government reports had documented the devastating effects of poverty, starvation, and social decay. George Orwell's *The Road to Wigan Pier*, published in 1937, would become perhaps the most well-known account depicting the misery of the depression in the north, yet, arguably, the industrial city of Bristol had already suffered every bit as badly.

In 1931, with rising debts and mounting pressure, the Government was forced reluctantly to follow the recommendations of *The May Report* and implement huge cuts in public expenditure, including welfare payments. At that time, *The Unemployment Insurance Act*, first introduced in 1920, entitled an unemployed person to claim a weekly benefit payment (then known as 'the dole'), for their first six months without work. The scheme also applied to women (although, initially at a lower rate, and on the proviso that they had not previously refused any offer of domestic work). However, by 1931, to help decrease crippling national debt and spiralling dole queues, the government implemented two notorious measures. Firstly, unemployment benefit payments were slashed by 10%. Secondly, the infamous 'Means Test' was introduced. Government officials made intrusive visits to family homes to assess their benefit entitlement. This often involved insensitive interrogations regarding family, income and possessions. Those with even meagre savings or a small additional income would find their benefit reduced. Tensions in Bristol ran high. For example, if the officials discovered that the mother or older child had a part-time job, or that a grandparent was living in the house rent free, the Means Test might result in dole payments being refused. Householders were also expected to first sell family heirlooms, such as pianos, picture frames, jewellery, or watches, before any benefit could be paid.

As a new year dawned in January 1932, and freezing winter temperatures bit, there were approximately 27,000 people in Bristol signing on as unemployed at the City's six labour exchanges (and probably many more who were unregistered).

Then, on 29th January, The Bristol Corporation – as instructed by the Public Assistance Committee – introduced the anticipated 10% cut in unemployment benefit.

Once again, the poorest in Bristol would be among the worst hit and the recently formed National Unemployed Workers Movement (NUWM) decided to act. Four months earlier, they had already signalled their intentions. During September 1931, a delegation of 150 Welsh Hunger Marchers had arrived in Bristol to lobby a TUC meeting at the Victoria Rooms. The marchers, together with their Bristol-based support, were baton charged by the police and prohibited from sending a delegation into the meeting. Incensed, thousands of Bristolians gathered two days later to prevent a second baton charge on the demonstrators. It was a clear indication of the shape of things to come.

Returning to the winter of 1932, a decision was taken to march to the Council House, at that time situated on the corner of Broad Street and Corn Street, on 9th February (Shrove Tuesday). It was to be an organised protest. Demonstrators would take to the streets (as the aggrieved of Bristol had done on many occasions before) and publicly protest the cut in benefits.

The initial intention had been for the march to be a peaceful one, and the authorities were duly informed. However, as the day arrived, a police cordon stood waiting to meet the marchers. Officers with batons drawn and barricades erected intercepted the protesters on Old Market Street, as they headed in the direction of the council headquarters. The crowd was shepherded along Captain Carey's Lane – a narrow side road next to the old Empire Theatre and Cinema (now long lost under the development of the inner-city ring road), in the direction of Old Market.

By this time, the crowd had swelled to somewhere between 4,000 and 5,000 people, and police officers attempted to direct them alongside the newly transformed theatre, (at that time marketing itself as 'Bristol's New Super Cinema'). The cinema's proprietors, having recently invested heavily in the theatre, were no doubt nervous at the spectacle of thousands of angry protesters marching alongside the plush new auditorium.

The noisy throng, which included at least 3,000 NUWM members, initially stood their ground as constables, both on foot and mounted on horses, charged the crowds. Under the orders of Chief Constable Charles Maby, the officers drew their batons and attempted to forcibly break up the procession. However, the sheer number of protesters meant the police failed to gain the upper hand, as officers were jostled and pushed back by the outraged mob.

The protesters then surged forward in heated retaliation and engaged the officers. What would soon be dubbed by the press as the 'Old Market Riots' had begun.

Inspector Dyke, the officer placed in charge at the scene, would later state 'sticks with nails protruding were being thrown at and used upon the police. I then gave instructions to the men who arrived with me to clear the street. The crowd was very hostile and it was impossible for any traffic to get away until the crowd was dispersed by the policemen using their sticks.'

One policeman and several marchers were seriously injured, while a number of bystanders also required hospital treatment.

The view of the protesters was inevitably different, as one eyewitness to the carnage recollected that 'the police on mounted horses and other police with batons charged us and drove us back into Old Market Street. People got hurt, people who weren't even in the scuffle. I can remember, there was a man and a woman there, they were clubbed down. They said they had just come from the pictures. And they had nothing to do with it.'

The police made no immediate arrests around Old Market, instead preferring a policy of dispersal. However, protesters simply regrouped instead at the Horsefair where it was decided to march again two weeks later in a much better organised and planned demonstration. Even as this decision was reached, more officers had arrived from Bridewell Police Station, two arrests were made and the demonstrators were dispersed.

The action of the police had seemed heavy-handed to many. Councillor H. E. Rogers publicly stated: 'Surely your men have not been instructed to trample to death law-abiding citizens whose only object is to pursue the legitimate conduct of citizens!'

Angered, the NUWM – bolstered by successful demonstrations in other cities – organised another unauthorised protest. On 24th February 1932 protesters once again gathered in numbers, many carrying placards, and headed to Old Market Street. This time the result would be a more bloody and violent one.

Estimates of the numbers taking part in the demonstration ranged from as little as 3,000 protesters to as many as 15,000. This was due, partly, to the widespread presence of Britain's press, each newspaper's estimates no doubt designed to suit their owner's individual agendas.

Although Bristol Police had declared the march an illegal one, the NUWM was not to be discouraged. Initially, the mostly peaceful procession followed a circuitous route through Bristol's streets, although with a clear intention of congregating at Old Market Street. Once there, the protesters were met at the junction of Castle Street by a large double row of police officers, ready with batons drawn, backed by barricades and mounted officers. However, the marchers were blissfully unaware of Chief Constable Maby's plan to ambush the NUWM's ringleaders by concealing a sizeable force of especially trained officers, who had been hidden in an annex of the Empire Cinema on the corner of Captain Carey's Lane.

Those at the front of march slowed down, then stopped, on seeing the police barricade in front of them. Uunfortunately, the momentum of the throng behind forced the front rank of protesters forwards. The police immediately unleashed an assault on the ringleaders at the front of the procession. Simultaneously, the officers waiting, hidden, in the annex of the Empire Cinema burst out and surged forward, splitting the marchers in two. In the resulting confusion, the police endeavoured to scatter the protesters by lashing out with their batons, then chasing the fleeing demonstrators along Old Market Street. Despite the apparent panic among the marchers, there was an atmosphere of anger and determined resistance.

As they ran, many of the protesters stopped passing coal delivery lorries, and raided nearby scrap yards and street traders, grabbing handfuls of anything that might serve as a weapon or projectile. Handfuls of potatoes, cabbages, pieces of coal, bricks, cobbles, and pieces of broken baton were used as ammunition and hurled at the pursuing police.

The epicentre of the disturbance rapidly shifted to Lawford's Gate at the east end of Old Market Street. Fighting then quickly spread into the nearby areas of St. Jude's and St. Philip's, continuing for almost two hours. At least thirty protesters were hurt and several police officers required hospital treatment for lacerations to the face.

Photographers from national newspapers, such as the *Daily Mirror*, *Daily Sketch*, and *Daily Mail* printed images showing officers with truncheons, beating protesters to the ground, while injured demonstrators lay nearby, collapsed on the road, their placards broken and discarded, and bicycles abandoned.

Despite the authority's best attempts to disperse the marchers, the NUWM leadership called for protesters to attend a mass meeting on Welsh Back later that same evening. As darkness fell, around 3,000 Bristolians gathered near Bristol Bridge. Once again, a large police presence was waiting for the demonstrators. Hundreds of officers jostled the marchers who, in turn, taunted and goaded their oppressors. The mob then stampeded in the direction of Bridge Street and Castle Street, chanting, smashing windows, and attacking motor cars as they fled.

The following day, 25th February, Chief Constable Maby called an urgent press conference at the Central Police Station. Forced to justify the levels of force used by his officers, Maby invited Fleet Street's pressmen to photograph a motley collection of jemmies, batons, sticks with nails hammered into them, and metal railings – all allegedly taken from demonstrators (although many of the protesters firmly denied that any such weapons were used by the marchers).

Charles Maby informed the reporters that approximately fifty police officers were employed to disperse the marchers, however, the *Bristol Evening World* suggested that the number was closer to 300.

At a later Home Office review, Charles Maby reported that 'one procession proceeded through St Philip down Old Market Street, and another procession, at the same time, marched from the other end of Old Market Street causing serious congestion. A cordon of police was immediately lined up across Old Market Street and the marchers requested to stop. They were refused and were told they would not be allowed to march any further and must disperse. The marchers then attacked the police with sticks and banners, pieces of iron, stones and other missiles and the inspector in charge gave orders for the police to draw their truncheons and disperse the crowd, and after a short time order was restored. The mounted police were called out, but did not draw their staves.'

An example was made of several demonstrators at the Bristol Police Court. Twenty-two-year-old Edward Fletcher, and Clifford Dyer, aged twenty-three, were charged with 'behaving in a disorderly manner and assaulting a constable.' P.C. Bailey testified that 'on Tuesday afternoon a disorderly meeting was in progress. Missiles were thrown, and a stone, thrown by Fletcher, struck me on the cheek. While taking Fletcher into custody part of a brick, thrown by Dyer, struck me in the back.'

Both men denied the charges, Clifford Dyer testifying that 'the real culprit slipped away during the fracas. I was on the ground with my face in dirt with several constables on top of me. Fletcher told me that he was standing right by me when I was arrested and saw what happened too.'

Superintendent Barnes informed the Magistrates' Bench that 'the trouble started when a procession of unemployed workers insisted on going to the Council House by a different route from that to which the leaders and Chief Constable had agreed upon.'

Nevertheless, Mr. G. F. Jones, the chairman of the Bench, had little pity for the two protestors. 'While everyone has sympathy with the unemployed every section of this community has to confine themselves within the law and not become violent, it is impossible for us to allow mob law to become the condition of the day. You are both hereby sentenced to fourteen days in prison.'

As the prisoners were taken down to the cells, Dyer shouted out, 'If you call this justice, I'm done!'

Sadly, the actions of the authorities did little to defuse the tensions felt in Bristol. On 9th June, a number of unemployed demonstrators were injured in a police baton charge and taken to hospital. Approximately 3,000 men had gathered in the city centre in protest, after the Public Assistance Committee had refused to receive a deputation of unemployed workers on the vexed question of the Means Test. Police efforts to disperse the demonstrators were greeted with a shower of stones and other projectiles, and several shop windows were shattered. Once again, the police employed a surprise tactic against the marchers. At 10:30pm as the demonstrators dispersed, streetlights in the city centre were suddenly switched off. Officers (some on horseback) then emerged unexpectedly, and simultaneously, from several side streets, wielding batons, and charged the protesters.

Unfortunately, at the very moment the police charge began, hundreds of moviegoers were leaving the last showing at the nearby Regency Cinema, only to be caught up in the carnage. One eyewitness recorded that 'the street looked like a battlefield. Men lay prone in every direction and blood ran on the pavements.'

The Daily News reported that 'as police charged, the crowd scattered, leaving five injured men lying in the road. Women ran screaming into doorways. Seventy protestors were injured.'

Of these seventy, twenty-nine required hospital treatment.

The population of Bristol was shocked by this premeditated attack on the demonstrators. The Labour Party demanded an immediate public inquiry. As a result, Bristol Police switched their tactic from one of breaking up marches, to one of arresting the NUWM leaders for incitement to riot. Within a few weeks, many of the ringleaders had been arrested, helping to ensure the opportunity for any similar demonstrations largely petered out (with the exception of a small altercation on 9th August).

Following the Old Market Riots, Bristol Corporation agreed in future to meet deputations from the NUWM. In addition, the proposed 10% cut to welfare benefit payments was postponed. In 1935, the notorious cut in unemployment benefit was reversed, and the *Distressed Areas Act* was passed, which allowed for public-funded employment in many of Britain's worst hit cities.

Gradually, over the following decade, unemployment in Bristol fell. By 1937 there were just 11,500 people registered as out of work. The boom in the aviation manufacturing sector and the increase in manufacturing and shipping caused by the Second World War brought more employment to the city.

Despite the controversy caused by the police tactics during the riots, it did not seem to affect the career of Chief Constable Charles Maby who would later be knighted. He was also famously photographed in 1941 accompanying Winston Churchill and the American Ambassador around the bomb ravaged city, following the 'Bristol Blitz'.

MURDER ON WELLS ROAD (PART ONE)

As a cold and crisp new year dawned in January 1949, Detective Superintendent Fred Carter of Bristol C.I.D. was hoping that it would bring him a much-needed change of fortune. Violent crime in Bristol was rising. He had all but given up any hope of solving *The Odeon Cinema Murder*, which had taken place almost three years earlier. In 1947, during another trial (featured in the earlier story *The Portway Taxi-Cab Murder*), Carter had been taunted openly in court by John Dillon's barrister, over his inability to find the killer of Odeon cinema manager Robert Parrington-Jackson. Surely, D.S. Carter pondered, 1949 would bring him the change of luck he needed. His thoughts were interrupted at 3:09pm on Friday 7th January 1949, by an emergency 999 call received by the operator at Bridewell Police Station in the city,

'Hello. Something queer is happening. A rough-looking man has just rushed out of Lloyds Bank in Knowle. He's a young man, about twenty-six. I heard gunshots.'

The 999-emergency telephone service had finally arrived in Bristol in July 1947, after many delays and much public clamouring. Would its installation at last give the police the opportunity to respond speedily and effectively in the battle against Bristol's growing crime wave? There had been eight violent crimes in the city during the previous six weeks. Or, perhaps the new 999 service would assist DS Fred Carter in finally catching the Odeon killer who had now evaded him for almost three years. He grabbed his hat and coat, motioned to the duty sergeant to organise uniformed officers and two cars, and the men rushed to the Knowle branch of Lloyds Bank located in Wells Road, opposite the Knowle Methodist Church.

One hour earlier, just after 2:00pm, a black Austin 16 had pulled up outside that small sub-branch of Lloyds Bank. A young man in a trilby hat and glasses and carrying a dark leather briefcase climbed out and walked inside the bank. There were two members of staff on duty at the time, Donald Twitt, the seventeen-year-old junior clerk, and George Black, the cashier-in-chief; a fifty-year-old married man, Great War veteran, and a long-time employee of the bank. As the young man entered the bank, he did not queue behind the two other customers already waiting to be served, but instead leant against the small counter at the side. A fourth customer then entered. The two clerks continued to serve the customers, firstly the local vicar from St Barnabas Church, Rev. J.R.N. Johnstone, then the young female assistant from the draper's shop two doors away. The last man to enter, John Rowe, a dog trainer from the nearby Knowle greyhound stadium, thought the young man's behaviour was odd. Unlike the other customers on that busy Friday afternoon, all anxious to finish their business for the week, the young man did not seem in a hurry at all. George Black, the cashier-in-chief, thought so too. Always a stickler for good manners and etiquette, George Black insisted on serving the young man first, as he had entered the branch before John Rowe. However, the young man did not want to be served at all.

'Can I help you, sir?' enquired George Black.

'I'm waiting. I have an appointment to meet my bookmaker here, his name's Murray.' the young man answered, in an obviously fake American accent. 'I owe him money.'

George Black continued to serve the other customers and the young man continued to loiter by the counter. The two clerks glanced at the clock on the wall. The bank was due to close at 3:00pm sharp and all the day's transactions needed to be completed, and the bank cleared. At 2:40pm the young man walked towards the door and, opening it, he looked along the road, as if appearing to search for the bookmaker he had claimed to be waiting for. After first looking left in the direction of Redcatch Road and Broad Walk, then right towards Oakmeade Park, the young man then came back inside the bank. 'Perhaps I'd better wait a little longer,' he announced, before returning to his position at the counter.

As the clock ticked around towards 3:00pm, and the other customers began to leave, George Black came out from behind the counter and placed the keys in the lock of the door, ready to close the branch, and clearly hinting that it was now time for the young man to leave. Black addressed him firmly but politely. 'I don't think your friend is going to turn up, and I need to close the bank now, I have an appointment.'

The young man explained that he would quickly write a note to his bookmaker, then leave. He picked up one of the bank's pens and hastily scribbled a note on the back of a deposit slip:

> 'See you Monday at 2.
> Missed you to-day.
> Joe
> Waited until 3pm'

He left the note on the counter. As he did so, the final customer, John Rowe the greyhound trainer, left the bank. Rowe glanced at the young man as he did so, with an inquisitive and slightly uneasy look. He instinctively thought something was wrong. Unknown to the young man inside,

John Rowe had decided to remain outside the branch. He secreted himself out of sight in a bus stop, a few yards further along Wells Road, and waited to observe what happened next.

As the clock on the wall of the bank reached 3:00pm, the young man returned towards the door. He was now the only customer remaining inside the branch. George Black and Donald Twitt glanced at each other, clearly relieved that this oddly behaving customer was at last leaving. However, in a sudden movement, the young man turned the key in the lock, pulled down the blinds at the window, and swung around waving a revolver he had hastily pulled from his jacket pocket. Before the two staff members could react, the young man shouted in his exaggerated American accent, 'this is a stick up!'

George Black was small in stature, but tough and resolute. He had often told his wife, 'if anyone tries to rob the bank, I will fight back.'

This he did, moving bravely towards the gun-brandishing man in front of him. Three shots were fired into the body of George Black, at close range, and he fell to the floor. The terrified junior clerk Donald Twitt was trapped behind the counter. As the armed man moved towards him, he defended himself with the only thing to hand: three heavy wooden rulers, used to line the bank's accounting ledgers. He threw them at the approaching gunman, who surprisingly did not fire. Instead, he pushed the frightened clerk into the cloakroom and locked the door. He then methodically removed the takings from the cash drawers. Selecting only £1, £5 and 10-shilling notes, he quickly bundled his ill-gotten gains into his briefcase and calmly left by the front door, stepping over the motionless body of George Black as he did so.

Unknown to the young man, however, John Rowe had remained close by. He had felt slightly uneasy at the man's demeanour inside the bank, and had decided to watch for his exit from the Bristol Tramway Company's bus stop close by. Although the city's trams had run for the last time on the night of the Luftwaffe's Good Friday air raids in 1941, even eight years later the city's bus stops still bore the name of the Bristol Tramways Company, and many of the tramlines were still visible on Bristol's roads.

Just after 3:00pm, John Rowe heard the distinct sound of three muffled gunshots coming from the direction of Lloyds Bank. He seemed to instinctively recognise the noise and comprehend what had happened. Yet, no one else on the busy road appeared to notice anything untoward. Rowe ran for the telephone box on the corner and called the operator asking to be put through to the police on the recently installed 999 service.

'How can I help you, sir?'

'Something queer is going on at Lloyds Bank in Knowle ...'

However, just as Rowe was about to explain his suspicions to the emergency operator, he broke off suddenly as he turned and looked in the direction of the branch. The young man in the trilby hat was now leaving the bank, carrying the dark coloured briefcase he had entered with, and walking calmly towards the black car parked directly outside.

Rowe ran towards the car as the man opened the car door, challenging him: 'You're in a bit of a hurry, aren't you?'

The man answered calmly, saying, 'I've just collected a debt,' and tried to get into the car. John Rowe grabbed the car door to prevent the man closing it, jumping on the Austin's running board as he did so.

'Stop!' he cried out. As he did so the young man punched him in the face which forced Rowe to lose his grip on the car door and fall backwards onto the pavement. The young man then started the engine and, using the still open car door to hit the prostrate Rowe again as he drove off, he made his getaway to the south and out of sight.

Despite being dazed and shocked, John Rowe had memorised the car's licence plate and he managed to stagger back to the telephone box to call the police for a second time. Everything had happened in the blink of an eye. It was now 3:09pm.

'Police?' he said. 'A rough-looking man has just rushed out of the bank and driven towards the city in an Austin 16 car, registration number JHY 812.'

Although having a clear view of the commotion caused by the getaway car, onlookers outside the sweet shop, the draper's, and the ironmonger's did not immediately realise a robbery had taken place. In fact, Mrs Maltby, the proprietor of the draper's shop, assumed the shouting and disturbance had been the result of a traffic accident. Within five minutes the scene on Wells Road was a very different one.

DS Fred Carter and his team of officers were first to arrive. On entering the bank they found the body of George Black on the floor. A member of the public was sent to fetch Mr Auker-Howlett, the local chemist, so that first aid could be administered, although Black already appeared to have passed away. Meanwhile, one of the constables dashed back to the radio car and called for an ambulance. Sadly, it was too late. The chemist later told reporters: 'There was nothing I could do, he was already dead.'

DS Fred Carter, assisted by DI Melbourne Philips, realising that the killer only had a few minutes head start, gathered a hasty description from the still dazed John Rowe and the young bank clerk, Donald Twitt. Fortunately, both men had kept their composure. Rowe had shown extreme bravery, and Twitt was the son of a Bristol police inspector.

Their description of the assailant was radioed to all Bristol patrol cars.

'Man sought in the robbery and shooting at Lloyds Bank, Knowle: Age 26, height 5ft. 7 inches to 5ft. 9 inches, pale complexion, round face, wearing dark overcoat and trilby, carrying black leather briefcase, and wearing horn-rimmed spectacles, which may have been used for disguise. Driving a black Austin 16 Saloon, registration number JHY 812.'

Interestingly, the police paid little attention to the robber's clearly fake American accent. DI Phillips called it 'phoney', informing reporters that 'most of our spivs think it sounds tough to talk that way, having watched too many American gangster movies.'

A police dragnet was thrown around the city, as news reached DS Carter that the getaway car belonged to a businessman from Bath, named Mr Chappell. He had reported the Austin stolen from Victoria Street in Bristol city centre earlier that morning. By 3:45pm, news reached detectives that the Austin 16 had been found, abandoned in Belle Vue Road, Totterdown, just over a mile away. Officers rushed to the scene, but the killer had already vanished. The police placed a 'jury wheel' over the car's steering wheel (a protective device designed to ensure that any potential fingerprints present would not be contaminated).

Meanwhile, forensic experts continued their thorough examination of the crime scene, as reporters and curious onlookers gathered outside the bank. Initial tests indicated that George Black had been murdered by three shots to the lower chest and abdomen. The first bullet had penetrated his heart and probably killed him instantaneously. The second and third shots had been unnecessary. Did this reveal something of the killer's mentality? DS Carter wondered. The shots had been fired from a .32 calibre weapon, yet there were no cartridges left at the crime scene. Had the young man been cool enough to pick up the spent cartridges, thus removing crucial evidence from the scene? An audit of the bank's ledgers for the day showed that a total of £1,444 had been stolen, in £1, £5 and ten-shilling notes. Worth more than £51,000 today, the haul was a handsome one. However, possibly unknown to the criminal, the majority of the notes were from a newly issued batch and numbered in sequence, meaning that detectives would soon be able to issue a list of serial numbers to shops, pubs, and other banks.

The hastily scribbled note, written by the robber and signed 'Joe', remained untouched on the counter inside the bank. Although police immediately believed it to be a fake, designed to put them off the scent (no bookmaker by the name of Murray was ever traced), it was nevertheless considered an important piece of evidence. 10,000 copies of the handwritten note were printed, with the headline 'Do You Recognise This Handwriting?', and circulated to police stations and post offices throughout the country. More than 200 sets of fingerprints were lifted from the bank and the painstaking process of comparing them to the thousands of prints stored by the Bristol police, and with those taken from the stolen car, had begun. It had been noted by the witnesses that the young man had not worn gloves; therefore, one of the sets of prints taken from the bank must have belonged to the killer. In the meantime, county patrol officers stopped and searched any suspicious cars leaving the Bristol area, while plain clothes detectives watched all trains leaving Temple Meads station. The net was closing.

Bristol C.I.D. asked the public to be vigilant, while simultaneously warning them against approaching the murderer, stating that he 'might try to shoot his way out of a tight situation with a revolver'. A Bristol taxi driver telephoned

the police and told detectives that on the day before the murder he had picked up a young couple and driven them to a Bristol boarding house. The taxi driver was confident that the man perfectly matched the description of the murderer. The woman, he told police, had been dressed like a Land Army girl. Officers visited the boarding house; however, the couple had already checked out, leaving no forwarding address. Another witness was certain he had seen a man matching the official description walking into another, larger, bank in Knowle earlier the same day. Maybe the young man had been confused and entered the wrong bank by mistake, or perhaps he had changed his mind on realising how many customers and staff were inside at the time? Either possibility, the police conjectured, seemed to indicate that the would-be bank robber was not familiar with the area.

Lloyds Bank, frustrated at the lack of progress, offered a reward of £1,000 for the capture of the man responsible for George Black's death. Despite an extensive publicity campaign, the reward brought only a series of false leads and dead ends. Firstly, detectives were told to look for a twenty-one-year-old Irish man, possibly a 'traveller'. The travelling community often became the scapegoats for unsolved crimes. Next, John Rowe, the greyhound trainer, was whisked away by police to Brixton Prison in London to view an identification parade, after a man there was arrested following a house robbery in London. Both leads proved fruitless.

Meanwhile, other tantalising clues slowly continued to emerge.

MURDER ON WELLS ROAD (PART TWO)

As the investigation continued, clues from further afield slowly filtered through to Bristol detectives. Throughout 1949, and well into 1950, bank notes with serial numbers corresponding to those stolen from the bank turned up in Liverpool, London, and Birmingham. Officers also tracked sightings of a man matching the killer's description in London, Cornwall, Ireland, Birmingham, the northeast, and even as far away as Italy, but all to no avail.

A month after the killing, a puzzling note was sent to the offices of the *Bristol Evening Post*, who subsequently passed it on to DS Carter. The note immediately grabbed his attention:

'Look for a blonde lady whose husband is a detective,' who 'was seen talking to a man matching the killer's description at the bowling green club.' The letter also strongly suggested there could be a connection between the robbery and murder at Lloyds Bank to that of Robert Parrington-Jackson three years earlier at the Odeon cinema. The description of the young man wanted for the Lloyds Bank killing certainly bore several similarities to that of the man wanted for the Odeon cinema slaying; in fact, without the trilby hat and spectacles – which may have been worn purely as a disguise – the descriptions were remarkably alike. Were the police at last about to find the elusive Odeon cinema assailant?

Yet, despite exhaustive enquiries, the 'blonde lady' was never traced. Was she also the young woman in a Land Army uniform dropped off by a taxi driver on the night preceding the murder? A blonde lady was also seen loitering close to the bank in Knowle on the day of the robbery. Was she the killer's accomplice or 'look-out'? She was never traced, and that line of investigation also stalled.

In the meantime, DI Phillips, in answer to his appeal for sightings of the young man, had continued to pursue active leads originating from the Bristol public. Gradually, a picture of the killer's personality and movements developed. Several people had witnessed someone driving the stolen car in the hours leading up to the robbery. Obviously, the killer was not afraid to be observed in a stolen vehicle, nor did he seem to be unduly concerned about standing in full view of other customers for almost an hour in the bank. He was clearly sufficiently cold and calculating enough to gun down the unarmed George Black at close range (and perhaps the manager of the Odeon cinema too), then walk calmly from the bank in broad daylight, yet carelessly leave a handwritten note and fingerprints behind him. Was he completely inexperienced, an 'amateur' thief, prone to panic, or a highly seasoned one, able to carefully lay down a series of red herrings for the police, while outwardly living a respectable and routine life? Police and press theories were wide-ranging.

Over the coming days, additional details gradually emerged. After abandoning the stolen Austin 16, the young man had been observed boarding a bus to Bath. Once there, he had taken a train to Yate, then changed trains for Birmingham New Street, where he promptly disappeared among the crowds. Despite the trail once again running cold, several strands of evidence now seemed to suggest the quest for the murderer of George Black lay further north. However, detectives would need to wait a further eight months, until events 275 miles away in Alston, Cumbria, at last provided

Bristol C.I.D. with a credible suspect.

At midday on Tuesday 13th September 1949, a large saloon car pulled up alongside a small branch of Midland Bank in Front Street, Alston. A young man emerged from the car, wearing a blue suit, raincoat, and grey trilby hat, and carrying a dark-coloured briefcase. In a similar fashion to the Knowle branch of Lloyds Bank, there were only two members of staff on duty at the time; a junior bank clerk named James Rush, and the manager, Andrew Steele, who was working in his private office at the back. The young man introduced himself as 'Mr Johnstone', and explained to James Rush that he wished to open an account at the branch. At that time, the opening of a new account would have been handled by the manager, not a junior member of staff (the young man would have been fully aware of this). James Rush knocked on the manager's door and showed the prospective client into Andrew Steele's office, before closing the door and returning to his post. Less than a minute later, the bank's external alarm began to sound in the street outside, a gunshot rang out, and the door of the manager's office burst open. The young man ran out of the bank, jumped in his car, and sped away. Several passers-by in Front Street heard the noise of the alarm bell, followed by the shot, and witnessed the ensuing commotion. Meanwhile, James Rush, the bank clerk, found Andrew Steele slumped in his chair, with a .32 calibre bullet wound to his abdomen, in a similar fashion to that suffered by George Black in Knowle. The young clerk quickly summoned an ambulance and the local police. When the ambulance arrived, Andrew Steele was still alive. En route to the hospital, he was able to tell the ambulance driver that the 'well-dressed' young man had demanded to know how much money was in the bank. Mr Steele refused to divulge the information and was able to activate the bank's external alarm by putting his foot on a hidden lever under his desk. On hearing the bell, the gunman pulled out a pistol and shot fifty-eight-year-old Andrew Steele at point blank range. He died later that day in Cumbria Infirmary.

Fortunately for Cumbria Police, several witnesses had been in Front Street at the time. Mrs Alisa Sparks, who worked in the ice cream parlour opposite, witnessed the entire incident. She had seen the car pull up outside the bank, the driver walk inside, followed a few minutes later by the sound of a single gunshot, then the commotion as the man run out and raced away at high speed. Three electricity workers nearby also witnessed the getaway and were able to describe the young man.

'5 ft. 9in – 5ft. 10in: Aged 24-25, grey trilby, dark briefcase, glasses, appeared businesslike and respectable.'

The description was eerily similar to that of the man responsible for the Lloyds Bank robbery and shooting in Knowle, and word was soon despatched to the C.I.D. in Bristol.

Meanwhile in Cumbria, the local police officer, Sergeant Mounsey, was certainly not used to an incident of this severity, and he radioed area headquarters in Penrith. They quickly dispatched officers to Alston, one of whom was a highly experienced constable named Henry Inglis. Not knowing in which direction the murderer had made his escape, PC Inglis and another patrolman, utilising their police motorcycles, decided to sweep as many roads in the surrounding areas as they could, in the hope that one of them might spot the car. Eventually they came across a stationary car parked in a gap among the hedgerows on the side of a country road between Langwathby and Melmerby. Aware that the car could be the getaway vehicle, and the driver was armed, they took no chances. The two officers approached the car cautiously. However, there was no movement from inside the vehicle. The driver was dead, with what appeared to be a self-inflicted bullet wound.

Although several newspapers subsequently reported that no weapon was found at the scene (thus adding some mystique to the events and implying a third party may have been present), a German Mauser HSc .32 semi-automatic pistol was found lying on the floor next to the victim. DS Fred Carter in Bristol was informed, as a .32 calibre weapon had also been used to kill George Black in Knowle eight months earlier.

An identity card was found in the victim's pocket. His name was Charles Corbett Kennedy, formerly a classics scholar at Queen's College, Oxford, and a Captain in the Royal Dragoons who, despite being aged only twenty-four in 1949, had served with distinction in the Second World War.

An immediate trace was placed on the vehicle, which transpired to be a private hire taxi, and it was soon discovered that Kennedy had hired the car in Durham earlier that morning, requesting that the driver, thirty-one-year-old Ernest Ingram, a veteran of Arnhem, drive him to Stanhope. Neither Ingram or his car ever arrived in Stanhope, nor did he return home. In fact, Ingram's wife had been expecting him home that evening, as they had tickets for a local dance. When the taxi-driver did not return home, his wife had assumed he had been asked to work late. Ingram's body was later discovered in a ditch, on the roadside a mile east of Stanhope. He had been shot in the back of the head and his body hastily concealed under a pile of large stones.

Why Kennedy, the son of a grammar schoolteacher, a classical scholar, and army captain, had taken such a dark path was unknown. However, his description, the matching ballistics type, and the details of his crime, strongly matched that of the murder of George Black in Knowle.

Meanwhile in Bristol, DS Carter and DI Phillips became convinced that Kennedy must also be the man who had committed the murder in Knowle eight months earlier, and possibly the killing of Robert Parrington-Jackson at the Bristol Odeon in 1946. It was decided to send the three most reliable witnesses from Bristol to Cumbria, to view Kennedy's body. On Wednesday 15th September, Rev. J.R.N. Johnstone, Donald Twitt, and John Rowe – the three men who had all been in close-quarters with the assailant in Knowle – took the train to Cumbria, accompanied by Detective Inspector Aston from Bristol Police. On their journey north, the four men chatted and read newspaper reports of the crime. Rev. Johnstone noted that Kennedy had used the name 'Mr Johnstone' on entering the Midland Bank in Alston. Had Kennedy used his name as a perverse joke, perhaps to parody Bristol C.I.D.'s failure to catch him? Rev. Johnstone's name would have doubtless been familiar to Kennedy, assuming that he had followed the numerous newspaper accounts of the Knowle robbery. It seemed another enticing link between the two cases.

The three men viewed the body of Charles Corbett and, although eight months had passed, they all agreed that there were 'strong similarities' between the man they had seen at Lloyds Bank in Knowle, and the man who had committed the hold-up in Alston, then taken his own life. Contemporary newspaper accounts report that the three witnesses found at least six identifying similarities between the two suspects; height, pale complexion, respectable appearance, glasses, grey trilby hat, and dark briefcase. However, due to the passage of time, and the fact that the assailant had worn glasses and a hat throughout the two crimes, it was impossible to conclusively confirm that the two crimes were indeed committed by the same man. As Kennedy had taken his own life, perhaps in a fit

of remorse, or more probably, fearing the death penalty as the police cordon tightened around him, it would be impossible to prove his complicity in the Bristol murder at trial. Detectives were also unable to match any fingerprints from the Lloyd's Bank crime scene to the dead man, although they remained convinced that Kennedy was the man responsible for the shooting of George Black. The similarity between the two crimes, coupled with the fact that Kennedy's parents (with whom he lived in Morpeth) were unable to explain his whereabouts in January of 1949 – although they did confirm that he had suddenly disappeared for a significant period around that time – also seemed to point towards his guilt.

Bristol detectives were also left to ruminate over Kennedy's possible involvement in the Odeon cinema slaying three years previously. Each of the three murders certainly presented strong parallels. In all three crimes, the perpetrator had been prepared to openly visit the crime scene at a potentially busy time of day, spending up to an hour on the premises, and risk being witnessed. However, if he had really travelled from Cumbria to Bristol, his chances of being recognised there were, of course, reduced drastically. In each case the pistol used had been a foreign one, which perhaps indicated someone who had served in the military during the recently concluded war. His general appearance and age had been similar to the descriptions offered by witnesses at the three locations, only differing in those elements which could be easily achieved using a disguise, such as the use of glasses and a hat. Although the murderer of Robert Parrington-Jackson had been described as 'scruffy', this may have been an attempt by the killer to disguise his appearance. At all three locations, the weapon had been fired at close range and the assailant had fled the scene immediately. Significantly, in the two Bristol cases, despite a description of the wanted man being printed in the regional newspapers, the killer had not been recognised by the police nor identified by the press or public as being a known local criminal.

While making his getaway in the immediate aftermath of the Odeon and Knowle killings, the murderer had also managed to escape immediate detection or recognition, probably meaning he was not a local man. On the night before the murder of George Black in Knowle, a man matching the assailant's description had booked into a Bristol boarding house and, immediately afterwards, the same man was witnessed catching a bus, and then a train north. Both incidents strongly suggest the wanted man was not from the Bristol area.

In addition to the Odeon cinema killing, DS Carter was certain that Charles Corbett Kennedy was the man responsible for the death of Andrew Steele in Knowle. The circumstantial evidence and similarities between the two cases were certainly strong. Although psychological profiling as a tool of police detection did not exist in 1949, there was a concerted effort made to understand why and how a former classics scholar and army captain could have coldheartedly murdered at least three men, and possibly more. Kennedy's own father was asked this same question at the inquest into the Alston murder. Although he was unable to provide a definitive answer, he did produce the final letter he had received from his son a few weeks earlier.

> 'Dear Mum and Dad,
> I am going away. I don't think I can explain. I am too tired to try. Charles.'

As Kennedy had taken his own life, and with only 'strong circumstantial evidence and striking similarities', according to Bristol C.I.D., the opportunity to formerly link Kennedy with the Lloyds Bank murder evaporated. Under English law the legal position is that 'trials are neither initiated nor pursued against those who have died.' In certain circumstances – for instance, if the person had admitted their guilt before dying – a trial might be undertaken. However, as this is generally an expensive and time-consuming process, it is an extremely rare occurrence. Any legal attempt to formally convict Kennedy with the Bristol murder would have certainly encountered strong legal hurdles. As a result, despite a strong assumption by the authorities that Kennedy was also responsible for both the Lloyds Bank and Odeon murder, the case is officially still listed as unsolved.

Alongside the death of Robert Parrington-Jackson at the Odeon cinema in 1946, the murders still linger on the files of Avon and Somerset Police as the constabulary's oldest unsolved cold cases.

The £1,000 reward offered by Lloyds Bank for help in solving the murder of George Black remains unclaimed. It is worth more than £45,000 today.

The question of Kennedy's involvement in the Knowle

and Odeon killings, although never officially proven, at least now centred on the most prominent suspect.

Just one year later, in 1950, another suspect would materialise, albeit temporarily, when another Bristol branch of Lloyds Bank was raided at gunpoint. However, the efforts of this new bank robber and his companion were so amateur that they might easily have been lifted from the plot of an Ealing comedy, had the outcome not been such a tragic one.

ESCAPE ON THE NUMBER 28 BUS

A year after the armed hold-up and murder at Lloyds Bank in Wells Road, Knowle, Detective-Superintendent Fred Carter and Detective-Inspector Melbourne Philips still had a vaguely uneasy feeling. The number of armed robberies in Bristol had not decreased. *The Odeon Cinema Murder* remained unsolved. Although John Dillon had been convicted of manslaughter in *The Portway Taxi-Cab Murder*, the police had failed to prove a charge of murder against him, and Dillon's associates had walked free from court.

Although DS Carter felt certain Charles Corbett Kennedy was the man responsible for the murder of George Black at Lloyds Bank in Knowle, and a strong suspect in the shooting of Robert Parrington-Jackson at the Odeon cinema in 1946, if another similar robbery occurred, with Kennedy already dead, the investigation in these cases would be thrown wide open again. On the morning of Monday 13th March 1950, an urgent telephone call alerted detectives Carter and Philips to yet another armed robbery, at yet another branch of Lloyds Bank in Bristol (the third in a year). Although initially the incident bore all the hallmarks of the other violent crimes which had plagued the city of Bristol, it would soon descend into an Ealing comedy-esque farce – like the soon-to-be released film *The Lavender Hill Mob.* Sadly, its outcome would not be comic, but every bit as tragic as the previous armed raids endured by the city's banks and businesses.

Roman Redel and Zbigniew Gower were both twenty-three-year-old Polish immigrants. Both were unemployed, perennially short of money, and shared cramped lodgings at 67 City Road in St Paul's. The two men had arrived separately in Britain after demobilisation, and did not appear to have been acquainted prior to arriving in Bristol.

It seems the two men may have slightly embellished the story of their past lives, although both undoubtedly suffered during the Nazi invasion of their homeland. Roman Redel claimed to have fought with the Polish resistance, while Zbigniew Gower told his Bristol acquaintances that he had been a forced labourer working for the occupying forces. By early 1945, both men had left Poland for Italy where they joined the Polish Corp, attached to the British Eight Army, and fought against the German rearguard action. Following VE Day, they remained in the army until discharged in January 1947, eventually making their way to Bristol and taking employment at the British Oil and Cake Mills at Avonmouth. It was here that they made one another's acquaintance and, with much in common, a firm friendship was soon established. However, in March 1950, just a week before their planned bank robbery, both men quit their jobs. They had secretly plotted a much easier way to make a living.

Gower and Redel both regularly passed the branch of Lloyds Bank in North View, Westbury Park, and had noticed that the branch employed just one cashier together with an elderly guard. The two men quickly devised a plan to rob the bank on Monday 13th March, assuming that the cash drawers might still be stuffed with deposits from the previous week. They planned to steal a motorcycle beforehand, then make their getaway across the wide-open spaces of Durdham Downs, just a few hundred yards to the east. The men could then head either north or south along the Portway and out of the city.

To fortify themselves with 'Dutch courage', Redel and Gower indulged in a heavy drinking session on the day before their planned raid. Unfortunately, when they woke on Monday morning, they were severely hungover. Although far too intoxicated to steal a motorcycle, they did not postpone the robbery. Instead, they opted to utilise another form of transport. Redel carefully placed a .38 calibre revolver inside the pocket of his mackintosh, together with seventeen rounds of ammunition, and the two men instead hopped on a bus to Westbury Park.

After first hovering outside the branch of Lloyds Bank in North Viewnto ensure no customers were inside, the two men put their ill-thought-out plan into action. It was now 11:35am.

Inside the bank, the cashier Ronald Wall had just gone into the manager's office to make a cup of tea. The only other person in the building, John Bullock, the bank's security guard, was stood on the public side of the counter. Gower remained outside as lookout, while Redel entered the bank. Once inside the door, Redel quickly pulled the revolver from his coat pocket and pointed it at the security guard.

'Stay where you are!' he shouted.

Gower, disguised in a dark beret and heavy goggles, then followed his partner into the bank. At that moment, Ronald Wall appeared again from the manager's office, clutching his cup of tea.

Redel gestured menacingly towards the manager's office with the .38 revolver. 'Go into that room, both of you. Don't move for five minutes, this is a hold-up.'

The two bank employees backed into the room and Redel ordered them to raise their hands in the air, while he kept them covered with the pistol. Meanwhile, Gower scrambled over the counter and grabbed what he thought was a thick wad of banknotes and thrust them into his pocket. The two men then backed out of the bank, still covering the office door with the revolver. Once in the street, they turned and ran.

With the thieves now gone, the two employees acted quickly. Ronald Wall rang the bank's internal alarm bell while John Bullock bravely ran outside to give chase. As he did so, he grabbed the first weapon to hand – an empty milk bottle from the window ledge outside. Once in North View he spotted the fugitives by the White Tree, jumping aboard the number 28 bus into the city centre. He yelled out to the bus driver.

'Stop! There are bandits on your bus!'

Startled, the driver, Ronald Cutler, slammed on the brakes, jolting the passengers in their seats. Redel and Gower promptly jumped off the bus and ran off in the direction of Westbury Park Road. As they did so, Bullock hurled the milk bottle at them. He missed and the glass shattered across the pavement. The commotion caught the attention of several bystanders and they chased after the two escaping thieves. The bus driver and conductor also joined in. One young man in the chasing pack, twenty-nine-year-old Robert Taylor, was a veteran of the recent war and had survived the savage fighting at Monte Cassino. Although he now worked for the *Bristol Evening World*, Taylor was a fitness fanatic and a member of the Bristol Judo Club. He gained ground easily on the two escaping men and, although Redel turned and warned Taylor off with a wave of his revolver, Taylor was not deterred and soon caught up with the two fugitives. Redel pulled out the gun again, his finger poised on the trigger. As he did so, Taylor grabbed Redel from behind in a judo hold and attempted to wrestle the gun up and away from the armed man. As he pulled Redel's arm back and upward, in the direction of his own head, a single shot was discharged from the gun at point-blank range. The bullet entered through Robert Taylor's

right eye, passed through his brain, and exited via the back of his skull. Redel dropped the revolver and the two fugitives sped off, heading southward alongside the impressive villas of Westbury Park Road.

The heroic members of the public still chasing the robbers continued undeterred, while Robert Taylor was rushed to Bristol Royal Infirmary. He died shortly afterwards from his wounds.

Meanwhile, one of the pursuers, Peter Scarman, caught up with Redel at the corner of Queen Victoria Road. He grabbed hold of the escaping bank robber and pulled him to the ground. Redel shouted out, which alerted Gower. Gower then run back to help his friend. He punched Peter Scarman in the face causing him to stagger backwards and lose his grip on Redel. With Scarman temporarily dazed, the two thieves darted down Blenheim Road in the direction of Redland Green. By this time, several police patrol cars were also in pursuit of the pair. They were soon spotted running past a row of garages in Redland Court Road and were pursued by officers on foot, as the patrol cars attempted to cut off their escape route. After ducking down Old School Close and climbing across one of the gardens, perhaps hoping to hide in the outbuildings belonging to one of the large houses, the pair were finally apprehended on the corner of Clarendon Road.

The two fugitives were taken to Bristol Police headquarters and searched. The stolen pile of notes, hurriedly grabbed in the bank by Gower, was found in his possession. In his haste, Gower had made a crucial mistake. The pile consisted mostly of worthless deposit slips and receipts. The robbers total haul had been just £28 (approximately £1,200 today). Had the two men not panicked, and instead forced Ronald Wall to open the safe, they might have escaped with many thousands of pounds.

A search of Roman Redel's clothing revealed seventeen rounds of .38 ammunition, which matched the calibre of the gun used to kill Robert Taylor, and which he had been seen to drop during the escape. Gower immediately denied any knowledge that his partner-in-crime was carrying a firearm. Although Gower's claim that he expected the pair to successfully rob a bank without any sort of weapon, was not taken seriously.

Both men were charged with the murder of Robert Taylor. Gower replied, 'I have nothing to say. I have already told the truth.'

Redel responded, 'I don't believe it is true that I shot him. He was behind me. If I wanted to kill someone, I could have killed those two men in the bank and got away clear. I didn't go in to shoot anyone.'

Such was the public's outrage in Bristol that Redel's solicitor, Mr G. Hope Scott, argued at the two men's initial committal hearing that the case could not be heard fairly in the city. 'Few cases have attracted so much publicity, and before the men were even charged, the press printed an account of the alleged shooting. In my opinion, no member of the Bristol public could serve on the jury and approach the matter with anything like an open mind.'

The chairman of the magistrates seemed to concur. It was agreed that the two men would face trial for murder at the Wiltshire Assizes in Salisbury on 18th May 1950.

In the days before the proceedings, there was a dramatic development. John Bullock, the bank's security guard, received an anonymous letter:

> 'Bullock,
> You and Ronald Wall will get your just deserts if our two boys hang. We are giving you fair warning so as to give you plenty of time to wish all your relatives goodbye.'

The letter was unsigned and written in black ink, using block capitals to disguise the handwriting. Bearing a Bristol postmark, the letter was dated 23rd April. The sender was never traced.

Redel and Gower were given the services of a Polish interpreter at the trial, as Mr Justice Oliver opened the proceedings. Both men pled 'Not guilty' to murder. With several witnesses to the shooting and the botched robbery, there seemed little doubt in the two accused men's guilt. Despite this, their defence barrister, Mr Ewan Montague K.C., argued passionately for a reduced verdict of manslaughter. Gower's defence seemed to have shifted from denying any knowledge that Redel possessed a firearm, to not knowing it was loaded.

For the prosecution, Ronald Wall testified that 'Redel and Gower instructed me to "step backwards into the manager's room. This is a hold up." They backed out of the doorway of the bank, still keeping us covered, and said "Don't move for five minutes." After they had gone, I rushed round to the cashier side of the counter and set the alarm bell ringing, then telephoned the police.'

John Bullock stated, 'I saw the two men alight the bus and the man with the gun told me to stay where I was. He took the gun from his right-hand pocket and pointed it at me. The men ran off behind the bus across North View towards Westbury Park Road. Quite a few men took up the chase. One pursuer, Mr Taylor, got to within an arm's length of the man with the gun and grabbed him. Then the gunman paused, turned to the right and fired point blank into the man's face. The other man in the beret was just in front of the gunman. The pistol fell on the ground just a few yards from where the wounded man had fallen.'

The next witness, the bus driver Ronald Cutler, broadly agreed with John Bullock's evidence, but added that 'the gun went off while they were still struggling. It was about a foot away when it was fired. The man then dropped the weapon during the struggle.'

For the defence, Ewan Montague invited Redel to explain his actions to the court.

Redel declined the opportunity to speak through an interpreter, and addressed the jury in English. 'The first I knew that the deceased man was near me was when he caught hold of my arm, so I pulled the gun from my pocket.'

'And what were you going to do with the gun, Mr Redel?'

'Stop him.'

'Did you intend to fire it at all?'

'No.'

'How came the gun to go off, then?'

'When I pulled the gun out of my pocket, he was behind me and he got hold of the gun by the barrel and tried to take it off me.'

'When you pulled the gun from your pocket where was

your finger?'

'On the trigger.' Redel replied.

'Can you confirm for the court, you did not intend to fire it at all?'

'No, sir. I did not.'

'What result did you think it would have, pulling out the gun?'

'That he would stop.'

'If you did not intend to use the weapon, Mr Redel, then why load it?'

'I loaded it so that anyone I pointed it at could see it was loaded.'

'After you had robbed the bank, Mr Redel, why did you get on the bus?'

'It was the first thing we saw in front of us.'

'If there had been no bus what would you have done, then?'

'I think we would have run away in the direction of the city.'

Gower testified in his own defence, 'I did not see Redel take the gun out his pocket when he got off the bus. I did not expect him to use the revolver. When we were drinking on Sunday, Redel showed me the revolver but I don't remember if it was loaded or not.'

'Did you ever see any bullets for this revolver?'

'No.'

'Mr Gower, did you and Redel ever discuss what you would do if anyone tried to prevent you escaping?'

'No, sir.'

Following the closing arguments by both barristers, Mr Justice Oliver ordered the jury of ten men and two women to consider their verdict, issuing the following instruction.

'If Redel pulled the trigger, intending to hit Taylor, he is guilty of murder. If the gun went off accidentally, he is not guilty of murder, but guilty of manslaughter. There is no verdict of not guilty in Redel's case. If you find Redel guilty of manslaughter, then there is no case against Gower at all. On the other hand, if you find Redel guilty of murder, then there is a case of joint responsibility.'

While Gower had not actually fired the fatal shot, his complicity in the robbery and murder, under the principle of common purpose, meant the jury was obliged to find both men guilty of murder. This they did, although there was a strong recommendation for mercy in Gower's case. Mr Justice Oliver agreed with the jury's guilty verdict and, despite the plea for clemency, he sentenced both men to be 'hanged by the neck until dead.'

An appeal was launched; however, the Court of Criminal Appeal upheld the original verdict. Even a direct petition to the Home Secretary, James Chuter, failed to achieve any clemency in the case of Gower.

Both men were hanged side by side at Winchester Prison on Friday July 7th 1950 by Albert Pierrepoint and his three assistants. It would be one of the country's final double executions. These were banned in 1957, under the terms of the new *Murder Act*.

Peter Scarman, one of the men who had bravely chased the two fugitives, was presented with the George Medal, while bus driver Ronald Cutler was awarded the British Empire Medal. John Bullock, the bank's security guard, received a Commendation from the King.

Robert Taylor was posthumously awarded the George Cross for his bravery. His citation stated:

'Without any regard for the hazards, Taylor intervened out of a desire to help in the preservation of law and order and gave his life in a gallant attempt to apprehend an armed and dangerous criminal.'

In 2005, a blue plaque was unveiled at 24 Victoria Park, in Fishponds, the house in which Robert Taylor had lived with his family.

THE CLEVEDON TRAGEDY (PART ONE)

On Monday 2nd August 1858, as the light of evening faded away in the west, a sorrowful story of murder unfolded in the coastal town of Clevedon, thirteen miles from Bristol.

Twenty-eight-year-old Elizabeth Williams was last witnessed leaving a crowded Clevedon tavern with her two young children in her arms around 10pm. Elizabeth would not be observed again until the following morning, when she approached Police Constable Francis on the high road at Nailsea, five or six miles to the west of Clevedon. This time, she was alone and clearly in distress, her clothes and hair were wet, and she was shivering violently, despite the morning being a warm one. P.C. Francis noticed that Elizabeth was wearing neither a bonnet nor a shawl (an occurrence unusual enough to be immediately remarked upon in the 1850s).

'What is the matter?' P.C. Francis enquired.

'I'm making my way to Bristol, I have been looking for a police station,' Elizabeth answered, 'I wish to make a statement.'

A torrent of incoherent sentences began to gush from her lips, but the constable advised her: 'Wait until I have taken you to Superintendent Edward Jones at Long Ashton, where you can make a written declaration'. Once there, she made a full statement which shocked the experienced superintendent to his core. He detained Elizabeth Williams in the cell and, at first light on Wednesday, rode the twelve miles from Long

Ashton to the beach at Little Harp Bay in Clevedon. Here he discovered a small group of workmen on the beach. One of the men, a plasterer named William Somerton, was cradling the body of a small child. The unmistakable sight of another child was also lying on the edge of the beach, apparently washed in with the incoming tide.

Superintendent Jones, together with Mr Bruges Fry, the North Somerset Coroner, ordered an immediate inquest which was held the following day at the Rock-House in Clevedon (later extended and renamed the Royal Pier Hotel following the opening of the Pier). The efficiency and haste with which Victorian inquests were arranged and opened was essential, as this unique record of the proceedings and its requirements all too graphically outlines.

Within twenty-four hours, the coroner, superintendent, fourteen jurors, several witnesses, a doctor, and Elizabeth Williams herself were all brought to the Rock-House, to allow Mr Bruges Fry to open the proceedings.

'Superintendent Jones,' Mr Fry began, 'I understood that you had the unhappy woman, Elizabeth Williams, in custody at Long Ashton. I instructed you to bring her here, as I thought it desirable that she be present at this inquest, so that she may be seen by some of the witnesses also present here today.'

Having complied with the coroner's instructions, Superintendent Jones was thanked by Mr Fry.

In line with other Victorian inquests, all fourteen jurors were obliged to undertake a rather gruesome necessity. They were instructed to adjourn to an adjacent room, in order that they could view the bodies of the two children. As mentioned in the earlier chapter, *The Book of Skin*, inquests at this time were frequently held at local inns or hotels, which were often the only buildings able to provide a room sizeable enough for all the attendees, accommodation for the coroner and other officials, and a table large enough for the examination of a body. In addition, with no effective method of refrigerating a corpse, the necessity of arranging an inquest within forty-eight hours of a body's discovery was all too painfully apparent – especially to the fourteen jurors squeezed into that claustrophobic room at the Rock-House on a stifling August morning.

Even before the inquest had officially opened, the regional press had already got wind of the story:

> HORRIBLE DOUBLE MURDER AT CLEVEDON
>
> A tragedy terrible in character, and even more disastrous in its consequences, was enacted yesterday at Clevedon. Amongst the residents of that fashionable watering-place it has produced a most unwonted amount of excitement. The victims of this shocking crime are two children, who were both purposely drowned by their mother, who reportedly confessed to the police and was arrested on the capital charge.
>
> Of the many painful cases of murder which come before the courts of justice, this is perhaps the most painful ever heard. The prisoner, a young woman, is the wife of a journeyman painter, living near Bristol. They had been married four years since, and had lived together on the most affectionate and kind terms. She had two children, one three years old, the other eight months old.'

Meanwhile, at the inquest, the jury accordingly – and presumably reluctantly – crowded around the bodies of the two children. The notes from the inquest describe the

sombre scene as 'presenting a melancholy spectacle. They were fine healthy-looking children, and appeared by the placid expression of their countenances to have died without a struggle.'

With this grim obligation completed, the jurors returned to the inquest room and Superintendent Jones opened the proceedings.

'I am Superintendent of the Somerset Constabulary Force, stationed at Long Ashton. A woman, calling herself Elizabeth Williams, wife of William Henry Williams, of Number 2, Churchill Place. St. George's, Gloucestershire, was brought to my office by P.C. Francis (No. 133), who said the woman was desirous of making a statement. She then stated to me as follows.'

The superintendent cleared his throat, before reading the accused woman's statement:

"My name is Elizabeth Townley Williams (this is recorded in some official records as Towerley, rather than Townley). On Sunday morning last, my husband was cool and unkind to me, in consequence of my not having paid some of the poor law taxes; we had a few words, and I told him I would leave him, and he said I had better go. I remained at home with my children that day, and my husband, on his return that night, appeared cool, and did not speak kindly, as usual. On the following morning (Monday 2nd August), I got up and prepared breakfast for my husband and two children, and we breakfasted together. He was then kind to me. On leaving the house to go to his work he kissed the two children, and after he was gone I dressed the children and took them out, with a view to carry out my threat of leaving him. I went to the Bristol and Exeter Railway station in Bristol, and took tickets for Clevedon, and left with my children by the ten minutes to three o'clock train, arriving at Clevedon about four o'clock that afternoon.

As soon as I got to Clevedon I went to a shop near the station and bought a tart and some gingerbread. I wandered about Clevedon till eight or nine o'clock. and then went into a beerhouse near the Bristol Hotel, and had a glass of beer. I then walked about the town and round the beach, I think until about ten o'clock. I sat on a stone seat near the beach, facing the water, and my two children went to sleep in my arms. I walked down the sands and met the tide with my two children in my arms. Before I went into the water I put my bonnet and mantle on the sands. Then I walked some distance into the sea with the children still asleep in my arms. I then walked back up the beach, leaving my two children in the water. Next, I went and sat on a bench to watch and see if my children were washed ashore. I waited some time, but never saw them after that.

I also wrote a letter to my husband, which I placed on the beach. I then walked away. I had not gone far when I saw two boys standing with a light at a stable door, not too distant from the spot. I heard one of the boys say, 'that woman is mad', but I did not speak to them. I then walked on the road to Long Ashton."

Superintendent Jones put down Elizabeth's confession and, after a moment's pause, continued his evidence.

'I then rode the twelve miles to Clevedon; and found that the two bodies of the children had been washed in by the tide and had been found by a man named William Somerton, a plasterer. I ordered that they be conveyed to Rock-House, that they may be viewed by the Jury. The bonnet and mantle belonging to the woman were also found on the beach. I then charged Elizabeth Williams with the wilful murder of her two children, Elizabeth Townley Williams junior (aged three) and William John Williams (aged eight months).'

Mr Fry, the coroner, then spoke, 'Thank you, Superintendent. Could you please describe exactly what happened when the woman was first brought before you at Long Ashton?'

'Yes, sir. When she came to me, she was without a bonnet or mantle; her clothes were saturated with mud and water, and her boots and likewise her stockings were covered with mud. Before I heard the declaration made by her, and before I had heard the facts from Constable Francis, I told the woman it would be best if any statement be taken down in writing. I told her to be careful what she said, and she replied that she was anxious to make the statement.'

The next witness to be called at the inquest was William Henry Williams, the husband of the accused woman and father of the two children. Initially, Mr Williams could not be located. He had deliberately waited outside the Rock-House, as his distress was so acute. Although first refusing to enter and give evidence, he was reluctantly persuaded to do so by the coroner.

After being given a moment to compose himself, he

testified in a hesitant and emotional manner:

'I am William Henry Williams. Elizabeth Townley Williams and William John Williams were my children. The bonnet and mantle you have shown to me belong to my wife.'

'When did you last see your wife?'

'I last saw my wife on Monday morning, the 2nd inst., at eight o'clock in the morning. My wife was troubled with fits, and I have been in London following my business as a painter these past few days. We have been married four years next Sunday, and have lived happily. I cannot give any reason why she should have committed these acts. We have had no altercation, except there was a poor-rate which ought to have been paid three weeks ago. She told me she had paid it, and I asked her for the receipt. She said that Mr. Hunt, the tax-gatherer, would call with the receipt and bring the change. I asked her again the following Monday night if he had brought the receipt, and she said no, so I desired her to call for it. That is it.'

William Somerton gave evidence next. 'I am a tiler and plasterer living at Clevedon, sir. On Wednesday, at about half-past one o'clock, I picked up the body of Elizabeth Townley Williams on Little Harp beach. There were no marks or bruises on the body. Dr Theodore Davis was also there and he examined the body, which was quite dead. A man named Henry James was with me, and, in my presence, he picked up the body of the boy. We also picked up the woman's bonnet and mantle, and also a little girl's bonnet.'

Next to be called to give evidence was Mr Lysond Williams, the accused woman's father-in-law. 'I am a painter, and live in Bristol, sir. The deceased children were my grandchildren. I last saw Elizabeth Williams, – their mother – at twenty-five minutes past eight o'clock on Monday, in Temple Street, Bristol, which is the direct road to the Bristol and Exeter

Railway Station. She had her two children with her. I asked her what brought her on that road, and she replied, "I am only going for a walk." I never saw her afterwards. I did notice that she had her head cast down, and she seemed sorrowful. I told her I must go, as I wanted to see Mr Trickey about some money, and I wished her a good morning. She then went on in the direction of the Bristol and Exeter Railway.'

Millicent Salmon was then called into the room.

'I am the wife of Charles Salmon, a tavern-keeper, of Clevedon, sir. I saw the prisoner in my husband's bar at about eight o'clock on Monday night; she had two children with her; one of them appeared to be about three years old, and the other about ten months. She asked for a glass of beer, and sat about five minutes with her children, drank the beer, and gave her children some cakes. Our tavern is about three-quarters of a mile from the spot where the bodies were found. She was not excitable, and I had not the least reason to believe that she intended any harm to her children, as she appeared fond of them.'

The medical evidence was supplied by Dr Theodore Davis; and delivered with little consideration for the children's father who wept openly in the corner of the crowded room.

'I am Dr Theodore Davis, a surgeon residing at Clevedon. On Wednesday last between one and two o'clock, I was requested by Samel Griffin, the churchwarden of Clevedon, to go to the beach and examine the bodies of two children which had been washed ashore. When I saw the bodies, they were not in the position where they had washed up, when left by the tide on the beach, but they had been taken up by the men who found them and laid upon a bank away from the tide. I examined them as they lay, and had no doubt in my own mind that they had been drowned. The youngest child was a male, and appeared to be under twelve months of age.

the other, I should judge to be about three years. I did not strip the bodies.'

Mr Fry, the coroner, immediately ordered that 'The children's bodies be stripped so that Dr Davis is better able to examine them more minutely.'

After a delay while the doctor re-examined the children's bodies, he returned to complete his testimony.

'I can confirm, there are no marks of violence, cuts or bruises on the bodies as they lay, except a few trifling superficial scratches, which were most probably produced by the washing of the bodies against the pebbles. I am still of the same opinion that the two children were drowned.'

'Do you think that a postmortem examination is necessary, Doctor?'

'I do not think that it would throw any additional light on the matter.'

'The jury and myself are both of the same opinion,' Mr Fry replied.

Meanwhile, in the doctor's absence, Elizabeth Williams had been ushered into the inquest-room, followed by a considerable mob of spectators, who hissed and booed aggressively, as she was placed in a corner seat at the far end of the chamber.

Mr Fry then addressed the inquest: 'Dr Davis has finished his examination of the children's bodies. Police Constable Francis, it is now time to bring the prisoner forward, so that she may hear what I have to say.'

THE CLEVEDON TRAGEDY (PART TWO)

The inquest room fell into an expectant silence as a clearly distressed Elizabeth Williams was brought unwillingly to the centre of the room by Constable Francis. As she faced the coroner, Elizabeth pulled a handkerchief from her sleeve and covered her face with it.

'Remove that handkerchief!' barked the coroner. 'Recall Mrs Salmon.'

The tavern-keeper's wife rose from her chair and was again addressed by Mr Fry. 'Mrs Salmon, is this the woman who came to your beerhouse on Monday evening?'

'It is sir,' she replied, if you desire me to see the bodies of the children, I could identify them too?'

'That will not be necessary. Thank you.'

With that, Mrs Salmon returned to her seat and Mr Fry addressed Elizabeth Williams directly, who had again covered her face with her handkerchief.

'Mrs Williams,' he began, 'do you wish that the evidence be read out loud, so that after having heard it, you may make any statement you please? It is my duty to caution you that anything you might say will be taken down in writing and might be used against you, if the case requires.'

'No, sir. I don't want to hear anything.'

'Very well. There being no further evidence, it becomes my duty to offer some observations on the case. It will now be for the jury to consider how these poor children came by their deaths, so as to see whether a charge of wilful murder may be laid upon any person. In the statement made by the prisoner to Police Superintendent Jones, the accused woman distinctly stated that she drowned the two children herself, and all the circumstances which have been proved in evidence at this inquest appear to confirm that assumption. Members of the jury, if you believe the woman's statement, confirmed as it was, it is your duty to return a verdict of "Wilful Murder". I will ask the prisoner once more, if she wishes to make an observation, before I ask you to consider your verdict.'

Elizabeth Williams was less taciturn on this occasion, and answered, 'I have nothing to say, except that the taxes were paid; I paid them. The man took the money for the taxes, but I never told my husband. I was going to pay him some more money on the Tuesday. I hope he believes me.'

The inquest jury of fourteen then retired to deliberate their verdict. After a consultation of just ten minutes, they returned a verdict of 'Wilful Murder in both cases against the mother, Elizabeth Williams.'

During the coroner's pronouncement, Elizabeth Williams listened intently, and without emotion. She was about to be removed from the inquest when, suddenly, a booming voice from the back of the room caused everyone present to turn around in surprise.

'I am not quite satisfied!' It was the voice of Mr James Coddle, one of the jurors. 'According to the woman's statement she drowned them, but I am not exactly satisfied that she did it.'

Bruges Fry, with a strained patience, replied: 'Sir, I am always pleased when my jurors return a unanimous verdict, therefore I will explain the nature of the evidence and circumstances to you again.'

'Mr Fry,' James Coddle answered, 'I do not like to charge

anyone with wilful murder, unless I can clearly see that they did it!'

The coroner gently reminded the juror, 'Sir, you are directed to give your verdict on the children's deaths according to the evidence.'

Mr Coddle replied, 'All I have heard is someone here state that he heard her say that she did it, but that is all. That is not "evidence", as I understand evidence to be.'

This remark seemed to cause a murmur of dissention among the other jurors, one of whom ventured: 'Well, sir, I myself am of the same opinion – had not it been for the mud on the woman's boots.'

James Coddle, buoyed by this apparent support, spoke again. 'She might have jumped into a ditch on the moor and got mud on her.'

'Not that sort of mud, I fancy!' the coroner stated in an exasperated tone.

'Well, I am not satisfied,' countered Mr Coddle. 'But, unfortunately, I believe you have got enough without me.'

An infuriated coroner barked out, 'Mr Coddle, sir, if you refuse to sign the inquest inquisition, I shall refuse to pay you your fee!'

'Sir, I do not care about the fee!' came the defiant reply. 'I care about justice!'

Mr Fry ignored the errant juror's response and instead

addressed the room. 'Those gathered here can now see the value of my having summoned a jury of fourteen for this inquest. I shall record the verdict of the thirteen jurors who agree. This is the first time in my service as coroner for this county that I have met with such a disagreement.'

A verdict of 'Wilful Murder' was duly recorded, after a majority verdict of thirteen to one was signed by the other thirteen jurors; a rare occurrence at a Victorian inquest hearing, in which the jurors were expected to follow the coroner's instruction.

Elizabeth Williams was committed to trial at the Somerset Assizes in Wells and the large crowd eventually dispersed, as the aggrieved James Coddle continued to voice his opinions on the steps outside.

The bodies of Elizabeth's children, Elizabeth junior and William junior, were buried in the presence of their father at Bristol Holy Trinity Church in St. Philip on 9th August.

Mr Justice Baron Watson was placed in charge of the trial proceedings, as Elizabeth Williams was brought before the court in Wells on the morning of Wednesday 11th August 1858. The heavy rain and muddy roads did not deter a huge crowd from attending the proceedings. As was usual for a trial during that era, the accused person was forbidden to speak in their own defence. However, some additional detail had been added by Elizabeth Williams to her original statement, which was then read aloud to the court.

'I walked down to the sea with my children in my arms, still asleep, with their heads on my breast. I went with the intention of drowning myself and my children. I met the tide, and walked into the sea up to my waist, when I stumbled over a stone and fell backwards, and I did not know what happened for some time. When I came to, I saw something floating on the water, I got to it and found it was my little boy, dead, and I put it down again. I then saw my little girl in the water. I gave a scream and I went away.'

Elizabeth's father-in-law, Mr Lysond Williams, who had testified at the inquest, was asked to provide the court with further evidence of his daughter-in-law's family background.

'Yes, your honour,' he answered, 'I met the unhappy woman in Temple Street, Bristol, on the 2nd August. She appeared to be in a most depressed state. I have known her for twenty years. Elizabeth was frequently very strange in her manner; so much so that my wife had often gone and slept with her, for fear some mischief should happen. It was the dying request of Elizabeth's mother that my wife should do this.

'Elizabeth has often been subject to violent fits,' he continued, 'both before and since her marriage. As these fits came on, she complained of pains in her head. She became insensible and struggled violently. She would foam at the mouth, and her eyes would swell during these fits. I have often seen her change her manner, making me quite alarmed about her, and had paid a boy to watch her walk home. She was dotingly fond of her husband and children. I was told by her family that Elizabeth's mother and grandfather were also subject to fits of temporary insanity. Her grandfather ultimately committed suicide by drowning himself. Her sister, who is still living, was very strange in her manner and her younger sister, who has since died, was similarly afflicted. Elizabeth's mother was a person of weak intellect. When her mother passed, Elizabeth became much affected, and she became stranger than ever in her manner. Even since her little boy was drowned last month, she still believes she is nursing him.'

The painful testimony, which visibly affected all those in the courtroom, also proved to be the final straw for Mr Justice

Baron Watson, who called an abrupt end to the proceedings.

'Of the many painful cases of murder which have come before the courts of justice, this is, perhaps, the most painful ever heard. It shows the sensitive feelings of women. It is evident that the malady is hereditary, and the jury must acquit this poor woman on the grounds of insanity.'

A verdict of 'Not Guilty on grounds of being insane at the time of the crime' was accordingly reached by the all-male jury and Elizabeth Williams was taken down to the cells, to be transferred to Cardiff Prison.

Once again, Elizabeth's bewildered and distraught husband had felt unable to attend the proceeding and was sheltering from the heavy rain under the arches outside the courthouse. As the gallery emptied after the trial, he was consoled by members of public as they left. He muttered forlornly to anyone willing to listen to him:

'I did not scold my wife, I merely told her she had acted wrong in paying some taxes without taking a receipt, but her feelings were so sensitive that she could not bear the idea of doing anything of which I disapproved.'

Cases of infanticide often created a moral dilemma for Victorian courts. The need to dispense justice, while balancing the establishment's moral outrage with the general public's compassion, often resulted in verdicts of 'Not guilty on grounds of insanity.' Of course, 'insanity' in reality meant a catch-all clause used to label (without understanding or investigation) any form of mental illness. This usually resulted in confinement at a mental asylum, in which the conditions were often every bit as harsh as those of a female prison. Thankfully, comparatively few women were executed for the murder of their own children, although even the journey to that degree of enlightenment had been a rocky one.

Originally, an unprecedentedly ruthless criminal statute

– first enacted in 1624 against an unmarried mother charged with killing her newborn baby (or child up to the age of one) – had been used to punish 'lewd women' thought to have concealed their pregnancy and birth, then dispose of their baby. The law even carried with it a presumption of guilt, unless proven innocent. However, by the beginning of the nineteenth century, many influential figures in society had sought a softening of laws and attitudes surrounding this issue. Campaigners attempted to shift the narrative to address mitigating circumstances such as poverty, double standards in society, and inequality. A significant change in the law was finally brought about in 1803 by the passing of Lord Ellenborough's *Offences Against the Person Act*, which decreed that infanticide was to be treated in the courts like any other form of murder. A mother was now innocent until proven guilty. The tone of the wording also changed, diluting the definition of the accused person from a 'lewd woman' to a 'fallen woman'. Although, of course, in a male dominated society, the blame for any unwanted child was still firmly attached to the female.

Ironically, it had been the case of another Bristol woman, a young unmarried servant girl called Sarah Hawkins, which had helped to shape changing attitudes and legislation.

In 1708, Sarah had given birth to a stillborn, illegitimate child. She was then charged with her child's murder. Unless Sarah was able prove at her trial that she had made genuine preparations for the birth of her child (and not merely intended to kill it), she would be found guilty of murder and sentenced to death. The law at that time would automatically assume Sarah had killed her baby, rather than accept that the child had been stillborn. Sarah had been seduced by a man who refused to attend her trial and testify that she had made preparations for the child's birth. Sadly, his absence left her open to conviction under the 1624 statute, in which an unmarried woman who had knowingly concealed the birth of her child (which had subsequently died) was presumed to be guilty of murdering that child. She was sentenced to be hanged.

Sarah Hawkins appealed to Queen Anne, and Her Majesty ordered that Sarah be retried. A sympathetic public, together with a compassionate employer, enabled at least some clemency to be achieved in Sarah's case.

Her employer testified that Sarah had fallen down the stairs just one week before giving birth; and that this accidental fall probably caused her child to be stillborn. Testimony was also given that the child's body exhibited no evidence of violence, meaning it was unlikely that Sarah had murdered it. As a result, Sarah was pardoned – but only partially. Rather than being executed, her sentence was commuted to one of transportation to the colonies. Hardly justice, but at least she had given a voice to women in her position.

Although change was slow, mainly due to entrenched cultural attitudes to religion and what was deemed as 'acceptable womanhood.'

Gradually, as the nineteenth century reached its midpoint, insanity came to be seen as an acceptable explanation for the crime of infanticide. Three dedicated institutions were constructed as Victorian society's solution to this problem: Bethlem, in Bromley, Fisherton House, in Salisbury, and Broadmoor in Berkshire. The majority of female patients admitted to these three facilities were women who had murdered, or attempted to murder, their own children. However misplaced the treatments on offer at these asylums were, the law and the medical profession, at least, no longer condemned these women as incurably evil.

It was to one of these institutions that Elizabeth Williams

would eventually be sent.

Following her trial, twenty-eight-year-old Elizabeth was incarcerated at Cardiff Prison. Her mental condition did not improve and five years later, on 30th May 1863, she was transferred to Broadmoor. According to the *Lunacy Patients Admission Register*, she was described as simply 'insane.' Sadly, Elizabeth was never deemed stable enough to be released and eventually passed away on 29th January 1895 at the age of sixty-five. She was buried away from her children and husband, at St. John the Baptist Church in the Gloucestershire village of Coln St. Aldwyns.

William, the children's father, had long since passed away. Heartbroken and dazed after the death of his children and the trial of his wife, he moved to London but sadly died in 1871 at the age of just thirty-eight.

In the late-Victorian era, and even in the years leading up to the Great War, the plight of unmarried mothers, women suffering from mental illness, and those with children who they could not look after for personal or financial reasons, led to a growth in that most sinister and gruesome of Victorian activities – 'baby farming'.

Baby farming was the practice of accepting custody of an infant or child in exchange for payment. Women, often single mothers, who feared the social stigma attached to an illegitimate birth, or even the loss of their home or employment, resorted to paying a baby farmer to bring up their child. Regrettably, this frequently resulted in appalling abuses of the child, and most infamously of all, in the deaths of hundreds of children. There is also a Bristol connection to the most notorious of all baby farmers, Amelia Dyer, who may well have been Britain's most prolific serial killer, and is featured in another book in this same series of real-life murder stories, *Jurassic Coast Justice*.

Although several acts were passed to further protect children, including the *Infant Life Protection Act 1872*, the *Children Act 1908*, and the *Adoption of Children Act 1939*, it was too late for the many hundreds – if not thousands – of children and young mothers, like Elizabeth Williams and Sarah Hawkins, who suffered through poverty, misunderstanding, cruelty, abuse of their social position, and mental illness during the Victorian era.

IN BRISLINGTON UNDER THE FLOORBOARDS (PART ONE)

It was June 1923. Stanley Baldwin had recently become Prime Minister and the *Matrimonial Causes Act* was about to be promulgated, establishing equal rights for women in divorce; allowing wives, for the first time, to divorce their husbands on grounds of adultery.

Nevertheless, there was to be no such equality in the household of George Cooper, a thirty-four-year-old carpenter from Brislington, near Bristol. His wife, Nora, was pregnant. Against her wishes, George instructed Nora, together with the couple's young son Wilfred, to take an extended holiday in nearby Somerset. George informed Nora that it would be best if she and Wilfred moved out of the house they shared with George's parents at 30 Montrose Park in Brislington, and into her parents' home in Cliff Street, Cheddar, while he remained at home and decorated their living quarters. Although only twenty-six, Nora was of a delicate disposition, frail, and quiet. She reluctantly agreed with to her husband's wishes, after he explained that the noise, dust, and fumes from the paint would only aggravate her condition. He also insisted that she should not return to Montrose Park until September when the baby was due.

The young couple had originally moved in with George's parents in Brislington following their wedding at Keynsham in 1920. At that point George had been out of work for several years. In fact, he had only regained employment in

January 1923, when his father had managed to persuade his own employers, an engineering firm, to take his son on.

As September approached, and the leaves on the trees slowly changed into the golden browns of autumn, Nora, now eight-and-a-half months pregnant, began to prepare for her return to Bristol. She was astonished, on the morning of Friday 7th September, to receive an abrupt telegram from her husband.

> 'Nora,
> Not yet finished the work. Please remain with
> your parents until Christmas. Everything
> will be ready then. Be in touch again soon.
> Love - George'

Although surprised, and perhaps a little hurt, Nora did not wish to challenge her husband's quickfire temper and dutifully remained in Cheddar with their three-year-old son. George did not witness the birth of their second son, Alan, who was born three days later on the 10th September.

Meanwhile, as the weeks passed in Montrose Park, several people began to notice that George's father (George senior) had not been seen for several weeks. When asked about him by anyone, both George junior and his mother Louisa invariably responded by saying:

'Oh, he's been sent away on business by his company.'

This story seems to have been accepted without suspicion by their neighbours, who were no doubt grateful for the unexpected peace and quiet. Father and son were well-known for their fiery tempers and frequent heated arguments.

Both George and his father worked for the same pattern-makers in Bristol, enabling George to easily explain to their employers that, firstly, his sixty-year-old father had 'become ill' and, latterly, that he had moved elsewhere and taken a less strenuous job. The family were quiet, shunned company, and generally kept themselves to themselves.

In December, Nora, Wilfred, and the newly born Alan returned from Cheddar and life in Montrose Park continued much as it had before, apart from the unexplained absence of George's father. Louisa Cooper seldom left the house; her marriage to George senior had been an unhappy one and she did not appear to be adversely affected by her husband's long and unexplained absence. As 1923 faded and 1924 dawned, George Cooper senior soon became a missing person that no one seemed to miss at all.

The situation might well have remained that way had George junior not become involved in a drunken argument at the White Hart Inn in Bath Road, at the beginning of February 1924. During a violent verbal exchange with other pubgoers (one of whom was an ex-policeman), George threatened to 'do the same thing to you that I did to my father'. The following day several of those present in the bar at the White Hart began to question George's words. After all, no one had seen George senior for several months. Neither his neighbours nor his former employers had the slightest idea what had become of George's father. The Coopers had become virtual recluses, shunning all conversation and barely leaving the house. Finally, a concerned resident of Montrose Park decided to report the matter to the police.

Superintendent Tanner listened carefully to the story. Rather than questioning or arresting George Cooper without evidence, he began to discreetly question the Coopers' neighbours – firstly waiting patiently for George to leave for work. Almost immediately the tactic paid dividends. The statement given to Superintendent Tanner by the Coopers' next-door neighbour seemed to tally closely with the rumours beginning to circulate in Montrose Park.

'I have not spoken to any of the Coopers for quite a long time, and at first I did not even know that Mr Cooper, senior, had disappeared. Then I remembered that I had not seen him for months. Both father and son worked as pattern-makers with the same firm of engineers in the city. They were rather strange people, insofar as they did not associate with any of their neighbours, but kept very much to themselves.

At first, it didn't seem strange that I hadn't seen him for months, as he left for work early in the morning, and in winter, it was dark before he returned home. He was a little man, with reddish hair and moustache, which suddenly turned grey a few months ago. They were a musical family; the old man could play almost any instrument. The son was also musical, and the mother could sing. Then one night the music stopped.'

This final comment sent a shiver down the Superintendent's back. However, it was not enough for a search warrant, nor for an arrest. He pushed the witness again.

'Did you see anything or notice anything strange at number 30?'

'Yes, Superintendent. George Cooper (junior) seemed very happy with his wife and child, but his relations with his mother were unusual. They were devoted. More like a brother and sister. She was only in her early fifties I think, and must have been young when she had him. He didn't even call her "mum" or "mother" but by a pet name "Jean". Then, one night, in September I think, I saw a dim light burning in the kitchen for several nights. I couldn't see inside, but I know something was going on in there.'

This ominous remark roused enough suspicion and concern in Superintendent Tanner's mind that he immediately applied for a warrant to question George Cooper and his mother.

Officers arrived at the attractive bay fronted Victoria villa on Friday 8th February at 7:45pm and removed the two suspects to Keynsham Police Station, where they were subjected to an intense three-hour interrogation. George Cooper appeared stolid throughout his questioning; however, Louisa Cooper broke down and wept continuously, almost collapsing into the arms of the constable stood by her.

Finally, George agreed to make a statement, the contents of which resulted in both he and his mother being formally charged at a hastily arranged magistrates' hearing.

'George William Cooper, you are charged on suspicion of having, with malice aforethought, murdered your father, also known as George William Cooper, on or about 6th September 1923, in the house at Montrose Park, Brislington, near Bristol. Louisa Cooper, you are charged with being an accessory to murder, after the fact.'

As the charge was read aloud, Louisa Cooper cried out 'Have mercy on me! I knew it. I knew what I was for. I can only say the truth.' George turned to his mother, urging her to 'Shut up!', before gently pressing a supportive hand upon her shoulder.

George Cooper answered the charge in a more considered, even serene, manner, 'I should like to say that it was not by malice aforethought. I did it partly in my own defence, because my father, I believe, would have killed me.'

The two suspects were then placed in custody, George at Horfield and his mother at Cardiff Jail (there was no female prison accommodation in Bristol at that time). As the pair were forcibly parted, Louisa cried out to her son, 'Have I got to leave you? Let me share it. It is my fault.' George replied 'Don't cry' as mother and son were parted.

At first light police officers returned to 30 Montrose Park armed with shovels, torches, and other tools. Utilising information given to them by George Cooper, they began removing floorboards in the rear ground floor room, which had served as a kitchen. Once the floorboards had been prised away, officers could then start the laborious process of digging into the clay, earth and rubble underneath the house.

At a depth of between five and six feet beneath the surface, officers found the decomposing body of George Cooper senior, encased in tar and quicklime.

The trial of George William Cooper and Louisa Cooper opened at the Somerset Assizes in Wells on Thursday 29th May 1924. An excited throng of spectators had already gathered outside the courthouse to witness the mother and son's arrival, the pair having been transported from Brislington in two hired charabancs.

The well-known Lord Justice Montague Shearman had been selected to preside at the hearing. Something of a high-profile character on the court circuit, Shearman's presence in Wells had helped to create a huge public interest in the proceedings. He had founded the Amateur Athletic Association in 1880, conducted the official inquiry into the Irish uprisings of 1916, and overseen the infamous Thompson and Bywater murder trial at the Old Bailey in 1922.

Returning to the events on that first morning of the trial, when asked, both mother and son pled 'Not guilty' to the charge of murder. For the prosecution, Mr S.H. Emmanuel K.C. began by reading portions of Cooper's statement to the jury, before then detailing the events of 6th September 1923 – the last day George's father had been seen alive.

'Although from outside appearances it was a perfectly normal and respectable household, the deceased man and his wife had lived unhappily. Their son has already detailed in his statement to the police that during a quarrel between his father and himself, his father attacked him with an iron bar,

whereupon knocking him down.'

Police-Sergeant Clarke was first to be called to the stand.

'Sergeant Clarke,' Mr Emmanuel enquired, 'what did the prisoner say to you when cautioned at Keynsham Police Station?'

'Well, sir, Cooper made a voluntary statement at the station, saying: "I came home, I believe it was on September 6th last, about 8.45pm. My father asked me where my mother was, and I said I did not know. My father said, 'When she comes I shall upset her.' There was a quarrel. Father told me about another woman he'd been seeing; whom, he said, he was bringing to the house, and I said, 'You will not bring anyone here.' Father stooped down and picked up a cast-iron ornament of a cow that was standing in the grate, called me foul names, and said, 'I will throw this through your head'".'

'And what happened next, Sergeant?' Mr Emmanuel queried.

'Well, sir, the prisoner's mother came bursting into the interview room and said, "Oh, I did it! I did it! Do have mercy on my son".'

'And after Mrs Cooper was removed from the room, did her son complete his voluntary statement, Sergeant?'

'Yes. Cooper then said that the quarrel got worse,' Sergeant Clarke continued, 'and that his father said he would throw him out of the house, and again threatened to strike him with the iron ornament. According to Cooper, as his father was stooping, the accused man said he kicked his father in the side and the old man fell forward, cursing him, and declared that he would injure his mother, whom the father also called a "swine." Later, according to Cooper, the father was sitting in his armchair looking at him through his fingers and said, "I will do tonight what I have intended to do for some time".'

'Thank you, Sergeant. That is all.'

Sergeant Clarke left the witness box and Mr Emmanuel continued to read from Cooper's testimony to the police.

'The prisoner's remarkable statement continues as follows. "Later that evening, while I was in the sitting room playing the piano, my father returned. I had my back to him because I was at the piano. I thought I heard footsteps, so I looked up and I saw his reflection in the mirror. He had taken his jacket off. He appeared to be sneaking up on me. I believe he realised that I had seen his reflection. He pushed the chair aside and he rushed at me and said, 'Got you, you bastard!' As he rushed towards me, he pulled out a hatchet from inside his waistcoat and trousers. I jumped up. We struggled for some time, and I found I was getting the better of him. I took the hatchet from him, and I felt it was his life or mine. Next, I found I had the hatchet in my hand. All that had happened between us in the past flashed through my mind, and in a fit of madness I hit father a blow on his head with the hatchet as hard as I could. He dropped down and pulled me by the hair. I fell on him, and struck him several blows. It seemed to me that my sight was gone, everything had turned black, and there was a red mist before my eyes. I had no idea what the result of the blows would be. My father was dead. I had killed him.

My mother had not returned home by this time. All I could see was my father's head. He was lying on the floor with his head smashed, and in a welter of blood".'

After pausing to allow the jury to grasp the significance of the accused man's confession, Mr Emmanuel continued. 'The prisoner's statement goes on to say that his mother returned about 10:20pm, and that he – the prisoner – at once told his mother that his father had gone out after a row. Mrs Cooper then retired to bed. The prisoner, in his own words, then stated, "I sat on the edge of my mother's bed and said, I have killed my father. Before mother came back that night, I put a sack around my father's head, and dragged his body into the fowl-house. There, I think, he remained for the day. I believe that I told my mother I had killed him. I told her not to go into the fowl-house."

That is not all, members of the jury. The prisoner's statement continued thus: "I fastened up the middle room door so that no-one could go in. Some days later, possibly a week, I buried him in the middle room about five feet under the floor. I told mother she was not to go into the room, and she never entered it again to my knowledge until the boards were laid down. As far as I know the body is still there. I cut out the stained parts of the carpet, which, I believe, I burnt. Last night, for the first time, my wife knew of it. She was away in Cheddar at the time I killed him, and did not know anything about it until last night.

My mother knew nothing about it until I went to her bedroom and told her. The hatchet is still in the shed."

Remember ladies and gentlemen, Police-Sergeant Clarke told this court that the statement was made voluntarily by Cooper, before he had been cautioned at the station.'

IN BRISLINGTON UNDER THE FLOORBOARDS (PART TWO)

The prosecution dismissed Sergeant Clarke and called the next witness for the Crown's case against George Cooper.

George Blackburn, Louisa Cooper's brother, who had been asked by the police to identify the body, testified, 'I knew it was the body of my brother-in-law, George William Cooper. I recognised his waistcoat and the fact that all his teeth were missing.'

'Thank you, Mr Blackburn, and I understand you also received a visit from the accused man, your nephew, on 29th January this year?'

'That is correct. He came to discuss and apologise for some misunderstandings which had occurred recently between the family. During our conversation George said to me, "There have been several upsets lately since father has gone, but I know he won't come back, for the simple reason I have put him where he can't come back." He appeared considerably agitated,' Mr Blackburn thought, 'and I gave him a cup of cocoa.'

'And, Mr Blackburn, what did you think the accused man meant when he said, "He won't come back"?'

'I wasn't sure, but I informed the police the next day.'

'Thank you. No more questions.'

At this stage, perhaps fearing the worst, Louisa Cooper burst into tears, and needed to be comforted by her son.

Given the chance to counter for the defence, Mr Watson

K.C. objected that the rules governing the acceptance of the accused man's statement into evidence had not been properly complied with. 'This so-called statement amounts to little more than an interrogation of my clients,' he protested, 'taken down without proper caution or without a solicitor being present. And as matter of fact, the defence intends to dispute the correctness of those statements.'

Mr Emmanuel was given the chance to answer for the Crown and replied, 'The prisoners were cautioned, and I submit that these cautions make their statements admissible.'

The Bench allowed the prosecution to proceed, but a note was recorded of the defence's objection. Mr Emmanuel was then permitted to read Louisa Cooper's testimony to the jury.

'Members of the jury, Mrs Cooper made the following statement at Keynsham Police Station:

"I returned home on the evening of the occurrence, about 10:30pm. My son was in the kitchen, and I said, 'What's happened?' He looked poorly and upset. He replied, 'My father upset things – look what he has done.' He pointed to the kitchen, where I saw the marks of broken eggs against the wall and broken crockery. I had left four eggs for their tea. I was just about to lay the breakfast things out for my husband for the morning, but my son said I should go to bed, so I did. My son then came up to my bedroom and, sitting on my bed, told me what he had done. I went downstairs and had a cup of tea and after he had explained what had happened, I told him 'I am sorry if you have done this to save yourself.'

The police visited our house in Montrose Park. They told my son the object of their visit, and he made a voluntary statement to the police. The declaration he made was the one in which he stated that his father attacked him with an iron cow ornament from the grate and afterwards with a hatchet, and that he killed his father in the struggle."'

Having finished reading Louisa Cooper's statement, Mr Emmanuel continued, 'Mrs Cooper was no doubt in a hysterical state when she realised what her son had told the police, and rushed into the room in which he was being interviewed, and told the officers, "I did it! I did it. Have mercy on my son." We know this to be nonsense. She did not commit the act. I submit that the father was attacked by his son with brutal ferocity, and that the son buried the body in lime to destroy evidence of his crime.

The statements also seem to show that the female prisoner was not present when the murder was committed; however, afterwards, she assisted in endeavouring to put people off the scent,' Mr Emmanuel concluded.

A final witness, Mr William Baker, was then called. He had temporarily lodged at the Cooper's home until 30th January 1924 and recalled a conversation with the deceased man, George Cooper senior, one evening in August of the previous year, when the soon-to-be murdered man had suddenly blurted out the following admission:

'I am in a fix. I have been seen about with another woman, Mrs Goodman from South Street, and I want to elope with her. But I think my missus has found out. I bet my son had something to do with her finding out.'

Mr Baker also testified to witnessing 'George Cooper purchasing a half-a-hundredweight of lime, two lots of timber, and a drum of tar, and when I challenged him, he explained that it was for "Putting down flooring. I want to put the tar underneath to keep out the damp".'

Next, the medical evidence was given by the esteemed Home Office pathologist Dr Bernard Spilsbury, who testified that 'The deceased died from shock, and a loss of blood, due to a fracture of the skull. I discovered that there were no less than nine blows to the skull, and that the body had been

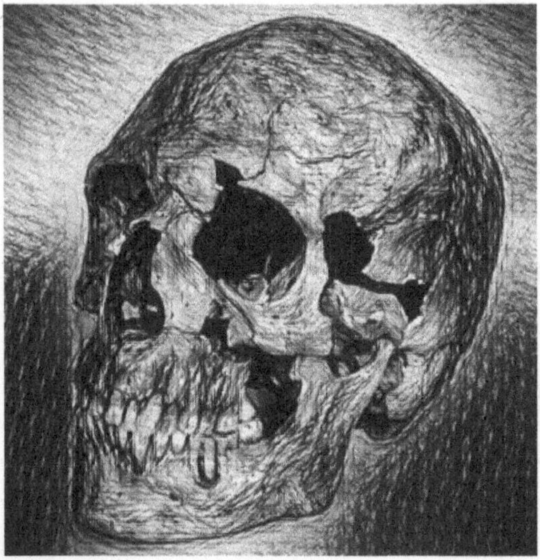

covered with tar and lime and then buried around five feet under the floor.'

With his usual dramatic flourish, Dr Spilsbury produced the victim's battered skull and held it aloft for the jury to examine.

That concluded the Crown's evidence, and Mr Watson K.C. then began the case for the defence by confirming that Louisa Cooper would not be testifying. He then proceeded to call his only witness – the defendant himself, George William Cooper.

Mr Cooper, please tell the court your story, in your own words.'

'Yes, sir.' Cooper began, 'I have lived at home with my parents all my life. I got married in 1920, and last September, my wife was away visiting her parents.'

'Now please tell the court about your relationship with your father.'

'My father was a man with a very bad temper, and he had no control over himself whatever. He once threw a brick at a man in Bedminster, and nearly killed him. On September 6th last year he left for work looking quite mad. On the evening of that day, the events that happened are the same as those that were read out earlier from my original statement to the police.'

The iron cow, which George Cooper claimed his father 'had picked up from the fireplace', was then produced as 'Defence Exhibit A'.

While her son gave evidence, Louisa Cooper sat leaning slightly forward in the dock listening intently to her son's every word.

'Please continue, Mr Cooper.'

'I do not propose to try and explain all of the struggle that took place. How I got hold of the hatchet I cannot say,' the accused man admitted, 'I know that after the struggle first started I had got hold of my father's wrists. I felt that he would take my life if he could, so I struck him and we fell over together. We fought like it was his life or mine. As we tumbled I struck him again, but whether he was on the ground or not at that time, I do not know. I knew then that my father was dead.'

'Thank you, Mr Cooper. But why did you not go to the police that night and explain what had happened?'

'Well, the condition in my head at that time was such that I did not realise what was the best thing do. All I knew was that there had been a tragic end to the struggle. I buried the body about a week later, in the spot where it was found.

If someone in the house that night had told me to go the police and explain what happened, I might have done so, but there was one to advise what to do.'

Cooper's honest and straightforward account of the tragic

events produced a striking impression in court. Several women in the public gallery were seen to wipe their eyes with their handkerchiefs and the female members of the jury appeared visibly moved.

Mr Emmanuel was then permitted to cross-examine George Cooper for the Crown, 'Did you find in the struggle you could hold your own?'

'I found I was not as easily overcome as I thought I would be.'

'Will you please answer the question, did you find you could hold your own?'

'To a certain extent, yes.'

'Did you tell the police you took the hatchet from your father?'

'I did say so.'

'You said you struck him a blow with the hatchet as hard as you could hit? Is that correct?'

'I hit him.'

'All the past flashed through your mind and you were in a fit of madness. Is that not correct?'

'Well, I do not think that is quite right.'

'But did you not say that, Mr Cooper?'

'Yes, I suppose I did.'

'Thank you, my Lord. No further questions.'

Mr Watson, then began the defence's summation to the jury, however he was interrupted by the hysterical Louisa Cooper who screamed out to the court, 'Oh! Save him! Save George! He did not do it! It is not true. It is not true.'

After Mrs Cooper had been restrained, Mr Watson continued, 'With reference to the female prisoner, to make her an accessory she must have done something to hinder or obstruct the course of justice. If Mrs Cooper did not help her son to bury the body, nor had any knowledge of the killing, she can scarcely be considered an accessory.'

Mr Emmanuel summed up the prosecution's case by stating that, 'The son hit his father – and I quote – "I hit him a blow with the hatchet on the head as hard as I could hit. He fell, and I struck him several blows."

Remember, the prisoner had previously said to his father, "My mother is not a swine, and if you say that again, I shall go for you". The son then buried his father's body in a pit and covered it with lime and tar. The victim was done to death by violence – and the man in the dock has confessed to having done it. Members of the jury, it is your duty to find a verdict of murder against this man.'

Once again, Mr Emmanuel's words were interrupted by the desperate screams of the accused man's mother, 'Oh, save him! Save my George!'

After the final arguments had been heard, Lord Justice Shearman summed up the proceedings for the jury, warning them that the exclamation 'I did it!' by Mrs Cooper was not admissible as evidence and should be ignored. The jurors were then instructed to retire and consider their verdict, while George and Louisa Cooper were taken down to their respective cells to await the outcome of the jury's deliberations.

The two defendants had a wait of only forty-five minutes before being summoned back to the dock. The jury had reached verdicts against both George Cooper and his mother.

'Do you find the defendant Louisa Cooper guilty or not guilty of being an accessory after the fact in the murder of George William Cooper senior?'

'Guilty, your honour.'

Lord Justice Shearman addressed Mrs Cooper, 'Louisa Cooper you have been found guilty of the charge, however, you were not present at the time, nor did you have any knowledge of the crime. I cannot be too hard on you for protecting your son. You are bound over in your own recognisances. I hope you are not required to appear again before this court.'

'Members of the jury, do you find the defendant George William Cooper guilty or not guilty?'

'Guilty of manslaughter.'

An audible murmur of surprise echoed around the courtroom, as Lord Shearman announced that he would be adjourning the proceedings for the evening to allow himself time to consider the jury's decision and the complicated question of sentencing.

The Court was once again crowded on Saturday morning when Lord Shearman began his address, George Cooper stood, unmoved, as he learnt the severity of his fate. His mother was noticeably absent from the proceedings.

'Prisoner at the bar, I have considered this case very carefully. I am always desirous of being as merciful as it is possible to be in cases of this sort, or any other prosecution coming before me as a criminal judge. But I cannot get over the evidence of Sir Bernard Spilsbury, who, not for the first time, has been of the greatest assistance in the administration of justice. He is always fair and always reliable. In this case his evidence was so fair that it was immediately accepted by the Counsel for the defence.

I cannot, however, reconcile the fact that the injuries to the dead man were most savage, and that is why I cannot treat this case lightly. I accept with compete confidence what the jury have said, that there was indeed provocation. But the injuries were most savage, and I cannot do less than sentence you to seven years' penal servitude. Take him away.'

George Cooper seemed initially surprised at his sentence, but quickly pulled himself together, and was hurried away by motor car to begin his sentence at Shepton Mallet prison. As the motor car sped away from the courthouse, several members of the public noted that the prisoner was smiling and chatting amicably with his guards.

George Cooper may have left the hearing with a smile on his face, but the remainder of his life would continue to be touched with tragedy.

Just a few days after he had been taken to prison, George received the news that his second son, Alan, had died, aged only ten months old. Shortly afterwards, Nora, his wife, also passed away at the age of just thirty-seven. A combination of her previous poor health, the strain of her husband's imprisonment, and the death of her son had proved too much for her frail constitution.

Several years later, following his release from prison, George moved to Mendip Road in Bedminster and volunteered as a reserve for the Royal Artillery at the outbreak of war. He helped to man the air raid defences on the home front, although his service was marred after he was charged alongside two other men for 'being absent without leave' and 'wearing the uniform of a commissioned officer, to which he was not entitled.'

After the war, and the death of his mother in 1951 (to whom he had always remained devoted), he married again in 1956. He was now aged sixty-six. Despite his new wife, Sarah Ann, being fourteen years younger than him, she passed away just two years later.

He married again in 1960, to Margaret Clark. The couple remained together until his death at Bristol Royal Infirmary in 1984, at the age of ninety-four.

His surviving son, Wilfred, too young to remember the tragic circumstances of his grandfather's and mother's deaths, finally passed away in 2017 at the age of ninety-six.

THE PARK STREET RIOTS

As the Allied generals began their tentative planning for the invasion of occupied Europe, the slow but steady build-up of American soldiers began in Britain. As early as 1942 the first troop ships arrived; by 1944 almost three million G.I.s were stationed in England with a huge contingent billeted in and around the Bristol area, mainly in barracks in Shirehampton, Bedminster, Brislington, Henleaze, and Ashley Down. It is estimated that between 8 and 10% of the new arrivals were African-American, somewhere between 150,000 and 240,000 men.

Racism was widespread among soldiers in the US Army, particularly those units originating from the Deep South, with many white serviceman believing that black soldiers were 'second-rate' and unreliable in combat. As a result, African-American G.I.s were conscripted into segregated companies and placed in non-frontline roles such as engineering, driving, labouring, or general logistical support. The US Army remained officially segregated and all military personnel were subject to the US 'Jim Crow' rules. These laws generally kept black and white Americans apart in everything from schooling to public transport. In the southern US states, shops and buses offered only segregated counters and seats for whites and blacks.

Although the British government did not officially approve of segregation, in military matters American troops in Britain were still subject to American military law. Bristol was seen as one region where tensions from such policies might well boil over. American officials suggested that black and white soldiers should only be allowed to frequent the public houses of Bristol city centre on alternative nights. Bristolians generally regarded this institutional racism as absurd and welcomed the visitors to the city. For example, in November 1942, Bristol Cathedral was packed for a special Thanksgiving service at which an American gospel choir was invited to sing. A survey of Bristol dockers in 1943 showed an admiration for their hardworking African-American counterparts, and in July 1943 a Jitterbug dance for Independence Day in Bristol attracted a multiracial clientele. However, the more extreme elements in the American Army still insisted that all Bristol pubs and dancehalls be segregated, leading to an increase in tension as the summer of 1944 approached. A number of Bristol public houses were politely pressured into serving solely white customers, while the poorer, less convenient, pubs often catered to Black G.I.s. Some Fish and Chip shops created a black/white queuing system, while others implemented 'White Wednesday' and 'Black Thursday'. Even the International Red Cross operated two segregated medical support stations in Bristol; one in Berkeley Square for white soldiers and the other in Great George Street for black servicemen.

Hoping to alleviate any conflict and, as an alternative to directly opposing the 'Jim Crow' restrictions, Whitehall instead made a half-hearted attempt to 'discourage' British women from fraternising with black G.I.s in Bristol. The Ministry of Information's West Region Advisory Committee noted that 'unofficial warnings should be spread about', using the Women's Voluntary Service as a conduit. A guidance memo issued by the Cabinet Office advised that 'For a white woman to go about in the company of a negro American is likely to lead to controversy and ill-feeling.' At an interdepartmental meeting on 12th August 1944 it was proposed that British women should be warned off fraternising with black G.I.s 'by an open statement on the danger of venereal disease.' By contrast, in Bristol, public attitudes on the whole were largely friendly and welcoming, although the Bristol Diocesan Association for Moral Welfare summoned Charles Maby, the Chief Constable of Bristol, to express concern at the potential for undesirable sexual fraternisations across the racial divide.

In 1944 the *Sunday Pictorial* published an article by the vicar's wife from St Mark's in Worle, near Weston-Super-Mare, in which she outlined a 'helpful five-point plan' advising local women on how to best deal with 'the threat offered by black American servicemen':

> Cross the street if you see one approach
>
> Move away if one sits next to you in the cinema
>
> Shops should serve them as quickly as possible, and,
>
> Make it clear that they should not return.
>
> On no account must coloured troops be invited into the homes of white women.

This article understandably caused a righteous outrage among black serviceman in Bristol and the fair-minded Bristol public. Tensions simmered as D-Day passed. On 10th July 1944 at the African-American billet in the Muller Orphanage in Ashley Down, a group of white US paratroopers allegedly assaulted and beat several black G.I.s stationed there.

As the warm summer nights continued, temperatures ultimately reached boiling point. On Thursday 13th July, men from the 545th Port Company, based at Sea Mills Camp, mutinied by refusing to attend a reveille parade, even when threatened with the Articles of War.

Two days later, on the evening of Saturday 15th July, tensions erupted again, this time in the city centre. American Military Policemen (M.P.s) attempted to enforce segregation at several public houses, causing a series of minor incidents as tempers flared. At the Colston Arms, on St Michaels Hill, the landlord refused to accept that black and white soldiers could not be served together. When several white G.I.s demanded that two African-American servicemen be ejected from the pub, the landlord declined, leading to a heated stand-off between the two factions. The fact that the landlord of the Colston Arms – named after the city's most notorious slave trader – was defending the black soldiers' civil rights was an irony almost certainly not realised by anyone involved that night. Aptly, the Colston Arms has since been renamed The Open Arms. While presenting a BBC documentary in 2015, Anglo-American writer Bonnie Greer noted that, 'There should be a blue plaque outside the pub – it was remarkable what happened there.' There were, in fact, no less than three public houses in Bristol at that time called The Colston Arms, a situation now happily rectified.

Meanwhile, news of the incident spread among the servicemen gathered in the city centre that night. Approximately 400 black G.I.s, who had congregated on the pavements and roads in and around Park Street and Great George Street, were taking advantage of the warm summer night, by protesting at their lack of access to the better pubs in the city centre. These had been earmarked by the American authorities 'For white soldiers only'. According to some accounts, several of the soldiers were accompanied by white British women. Some brawling broke out between a small contingent of men, no doubt intoxicated and still aggrieved by their recent treatment, and the order to draft an extra 120

M.P.s in Army Jeeps onto the Bristol streets was given. One armed US military policeman stopped a black serviceman and ordered him to produce his identity papers. An instruction was then issued, ordering all black G.I.s to gather in an orderly fashion and march back to the tram centre, where transport trucks were waiting to return them to their barracks. The sight of hundreds of G.I.s being marched down the hill to the tram centre created a chorus of disapproval from the onlooking Bristol crowd, who jeered at the American M.P.s. One white Bristolian woman was arrested after attacking a military policeman, whom she claimed had launched an unprovoked assault on a black serviceman. She was later fined for 'Openly causing a public nuisance'.

Perhaps emboldened by the support shown by the Bristol public, and angered by the enforced march, tempers flared. A number of the African-American servicemen wore holstered knives, and refused to hand them over when challenged by M.P.s. Their colleagues were forced to intervene after a group of over-zealous M.P.s attempted to disarm them, and in the resulting confrontation, panic ensued. One soldier appeared to stab a military policeman in the leg (some accounts claim 'repeatedly', others that the M.P. was 'stabbed once'). The G.I. was shot dead by another M.P., creating alarm, both among the large group of soldiers and the remaining military police. As the mob surged forward, M.P.s with automatic weapons fired shots above the crowds and low into the throng, shooting several men in the legs. One eyewitness later reported that:

'Some troops were walking along the tramway lines arm-in-arm with girls. They were stopped by a military policeman, who apparently asked for their passes. Then things happened suddenly. Some more troops came up and shooting started. One man fell wounded. It was alarming while it lasted. The civilians, apart from a few hysterical women who made themselves a nuisance, kept well out of the way. especially when the shooting began. Women who did try to interfere were bundled into ambulances and taken away. Military police in jeeps, armed with automatic weapons, rounded up the ringleaders.'

Buses were drawn across a series of adjacent road junctions, to create a bottleneck, and to hopefully confine the incident. Many of the wounded (either from gunshot wounds to the leg, or those trampled underfoot) were dealt with at the scene by St John's Ambulance Brigade volunteers. Those with more serious injuries were transported to Bristol Infirmary, alongside the 'more hysterical white women' who were removed from the scene 'for their own good.'

Order was eventually restored amid booing and jeering from the assembled crowd, and the 400-strong group of servicemen were returned to their respective barracks. American authorities instituted a three-day military curfew among its servicemen, with all leave passes withdrawn or refused. In total, the disturbance had involved approximately 400 troops (both black and white), requiring 120 military policemen, equipped with automatic weapons and army vehicles, to arrest scores of men in order to subdue the riot. An air of palpable tension remained on the city's streets and the resulting military curfew eventually lasted several days.

Bristol City Council called a special meeting to discuss the incident (which would soon be dubbed 'The Park Street Riot'). City Alderman Walter Hennessy requested that a statement should be issued by the Bristol Watch Committee to calm public fears and to avoid widespread newspaper speculation (which was damaging Bristol's reputation). He declared, 'There are many rumours flying about as to what actually happened. There is no question that large crowds of people were involved and that a shot or shots were fired. And

there is no question that some people were injured.'

Alderman Hennessy need not have worried. Two remarkable details were to emerge in the aftermath of the Park Street riot. Firstly, the overwhelming evidence of the openness and goodwill extended by Bristolians towards the newly arrived black G.I.s. In fact, the experience voiced by many of the African-American soldiers was one of surprise and gratitude. Walter White, the well-known civil rights campaigner who led the National Association for the Advancement of Colored People and advised President Truman on the racial integration of the American Army after World War II, noted that many black G.I.s in Bristol enjoyed, 'their first experience in being treated as normal human beings and friends by white people.'

Secondly, perhaps the most astonishing detail to emerge from the riot in Park Street on that July night in 1944, was the comprehensive and effective effort made by the establishment to suppress and censor the story. Indeed, were it not for the distance memories of those involved, and a less encumbered American media, little might be known about the events of that evening. Here, in the UK, the Ministry of Information placed severe reporting restrictions on the British press – known as a 'D Notice'. As a result of the complete news blackout no reports of the riot appear in any of the Bristol or West Country newspapers. No photographs of the riot were published, nor was any mention of the events reported on the BBC Home Serive or the local radio network. Nevertheless, two national newspapers did manage to somehow circumvent the censorship restrictions. Both the *Daily Mail* and the *Daily Mirror* included brief articles on their inside pages referring to the events of that night, although both editors were careful not to mention the number of troops involved, and to downgrade their description from a 'riot' to a 'fracas' or an 'incident'. The *Daily Mirror* also gleefully added that, 'The soldiers concerned in the fracas were not British.'

Thankfully, newspapers in the United States and Canada did not seem so reticent, employing a matter-of-fact style, as an effort was made by both the press and the army to establish the facts. On 18th July *The Journal Times* in Wisconsin, using the language of the time, reported that:

'US Troops have been forbidden to enter Bristol since a fight among 200 Negro and white soldiers there at midnight on Saturday. One Negro soldier was wounded fatally. Three Negroes and four white men required hospital treatment, army authorities said. White and Negro military police finally quelled the troops and placed four under arrest.'

Meanwhile, the *Daily News Journal* in Tennessee stated that:

'Brigadier-General Benjamin O. Davis and Major Homer

Roberts, Negro officers, were making further inquiries at the scene. Undersecretary of War Robert Patterson will issue a statement regarding the incident.'

On 29th July, Robert Patterson announced that an investigation was underway, during which it had been confirmed that, 'A number of Negro and white troops were injured. M.P.s were assisted by white paratroopers and Negro soldiers in quelling the disturbance.'

Yet, a month later, little progress appears to have been made. On 29th August 1944, the War Department in Washington reported that its investigation 'into the reported battling between Negro and white soldiers in Bristol, England, has not yet produced satisfactory evidence as to the causes of the outbreak.

Furthermore, no report has yet been received from Brigadier-General B.O. Davis, who conducted an investigation at the scene. However, according to information from the Provost Marshall's office, it appears that two Negro soldiers were beaten by two white soldiers, newly arrived in the area, without provocation. The next evening there was a clash between Negro and white soldiers, apparently a result of the previous incident.'

Needless to say, this second incident was not reported in the British press.

Almost as concerning as the lack of reporting of the Park Street Riot in the British media, were the rumours that surfaced three months later, during October 1944. A merchant seaman, whose vessel was docked at Bristol, and who had spent a great deal of time on leave in the city centre, reported to the Workers Defense League in America that 'white paratroopers had either killed or wounded more than a score of Negro soldiers in Bristol about August 1st.'

The allegations were taken so seriously that a discussion

followed between General Eisenhower and Walter White. Eisenhower cabled White to reassure him that, 'Pursuant to your message regarding incident involving the killing of eight and wounding of twenty colored soldiers around August 1st in Bristol, England, I had a thorough investigation conducted which revealed the report is unfounded and incorrect.'

If any such tragedy had occurred, it would almost certainly have resulted in a heavily censored local press being unable to report the events. The keen sense of injustice felt by the Bristol public would have undoubtedly been riled. Perhaps the second incident was concealed, or more probably, exaggerated by the merchant seaman. There does not appear to be any evidence to support his claim – other than a little reported and largely forgotten occurrence which took place outside Temple Meads railway station on Sunday 8th October 1944. A black American trooper, suspected of being a deserter, was shot and later died from wounds he received during a struggle with American M.P.s. The soldier was apparently in the custody of the military policeman when he struggled to free himself. Two shots were fired by the M.P. as the soldier attempted to escape. One shot struck the engine of single-decker bus parked nearby, the other fatally injured the fleeing man. He later died in the Bristol Infirmary.

Had reporting of this tragic incident not been so heavily suppressed, Bristol may well have endured, not one, but two riots that year.

THE TEMPLE MURDER (PART ONE)

On Saturday 19th March 1904, Bristol police received an urgent telegram from their counterparts in Salford informing them that they had taken a 'seafaring Bristolian' into custody on a charge of passing a counterfeit banknote. While being arrested, according to Salford detectives, the man had initially given a false name. However, when questioned, he now claimed to be Frederick William Hayball, 'The Temple Murderer', wanted for the murder of his wife in Bristol, almost five years earlier. Hayball had been on the run since 1899, having vanished into thin air minutes after his wife's body had been discovered. Despite several reported sightings, Hayball had remained at large, thwarting the best efforts of Bristol police. The only Bristol officer who knew Hayball by sight, Detective-Sergeant Churchill, was quickly despatched by train to Manchester. Was the five-year quest for 'The Temple Murderer' over at last?

Frederick Hayball was born in Bristol in 1864. Like so many others brought up close to the docks he became a sailor. In 1886, then aged twenty-two, he married a local girl, eighteen-year-old Ellen Milsom, at the church of St Philip and St Jacob in Clifton. Unhappily, the marriage was a violent one. Despite being away at sea for long stretches, Hayball managed to inflict a shocking number of injuries on his poor wife during their brief time together. Within a few weeks of their wedding he received a fortnight's prison sentence for 'wife-beating and assaulting his mother-in-law'.

Perhaps the only thing that kept Ellen alive in those early years were the long periods her abusive husband spent at sea. During this time, she lived with her mother in Hereford Street, Bedminster. However, she returned dutifully to her husband whenever he returned home on shore leave.

By the early 1890s, Hayball had grown tired of the sailor's life and instead took employment as a longshoreman at Bristol docks. Now living at home on a permanent basis, his excessive drinking and ferocious temper only escalated his violent behaviour towards Ellen and their young daughter, Mary. In 1892 Hayball was imprisoned for three months for 'beating his wife'. On the day he was released he again beat her, leaving Ellen no choice but to defend herself with a knife. Not surprisingly, she began to fear for her life and eventually left her husband, taking Mary with her. Ellen returned to live with her mother and took in work as a seamstress to make ends meet. At this stage, Hayball does not seem to have made any attempt at reconciliation with his wife. Instead, he signed up as a crewmember on two successive round-the-world sea voyages onboard a vessel bound for San Francisco, via Australia (Hayball's knowledge of these destinations would later play an important part in the development of the story).

Only after an absence from home of three years, did he visit Ellen and persuade her to move back home with him once again. Initially their reunion appears to have been successful, outwardly at least. Hayball continued to work as a longshoreman and Ellen gave birth to four more children; Frederick junior (who continued to live with the couple), and three others, one of whom was sent to live with an aunt, one was adopted, and the other taken into a children's home in Cumberland Street, known as the Guardian House. The couple rented a small two-bedroomed cottage in Jones's Court, a cramped courtyard of rundown houses located through a narrow and dimly lit arch, off Avon Street.

Although Avon Street is much changed today, it was once home to the gasworks, myriads of tightly packed cottages, and several nearby public houses. Hayball appears to have begun drinking heavily again and regularly frequented The Stag and Hounds, The Volunteer Tavern, and the Cross Guns Public House in Temple Street. Arguments erupted again between the couple, as Ellen struggled to raise their two children. Once again Hayball, a large and intimidating figure, became physically abusive. Ellen threatened to call the police, to which Hayball responded, 'If I thought you was going up against me again, I will out with a knife and cut your throat now!'

Finally, six weeks before Ellen's death, a summons for Hayball's arrest was issued 'For the ill-treatment of his wife.' He failed to answer the summons, and somehow managed to avoid arrest until matters came to a head on the evening of Friday 19th May 1899, when Ellen met her estranged husband to beg for some housekeeping money and to warn him that she was going to attempt an abortion. It seems that he again assaulted her, as she was seen that night in the street at 11:15pm, by P.C. James Smith. She was holding a child in her arms and displayed more than one bruise. She told the constable that Hayball had accused her of consorting with other men, and had vowed to call on her the next day.

The following morning, it appears that Ellen was still worried about her husband's impending visit, and expressed her concerns to a neighbour, Mrs Laura Gilks. So great were her fears, in fact, that Ellen informed her neighbour that she expected to be 'shortly unwell at the hands of her husband', and that she had obtained a key to an empty house in the courtyard and would retreat there with the children if her husband became violent. So anxious was Ellen, that she asked Mrs Gilks to 'call on me Sunday at noon, at the empty house, if you do not see me about first.'

By Saturday afternoon, after no doubt first stopping to fortify himself in one of the nearby public houses, Frederick Hayball walked under the narrow arch into Jones's Court. Ignoring his daughter, who was playing in the cramped courtyard, he strode purposefully in through the door of their lodgings. Once inside, he picked up a small hatchet from the back kitchen. Ellen, on hearing him enter, vainly attempted to lock herself in the bedroom. Unfortunately, he proved too powerful and rained down a series of hatchet-blows on his defenceless wife. A passer-by on Avon Street, Albert Flay, who knew Frederick Hayball by sight and had seen him enter the courtyard that morning, together with the other women who lived in Jones's Court, all heard screams coming from Ellen Hayball's home. Life was hard in Avon Street, with each family eking out an existence as best they could. Domestic incidents were sadly commonplace, and the other women in the courtyard certainly had no wish to interfere in another family's heated argument. Had they done so, Ellen Hayball might well have survived.

Later, the courtyard fell silent and life returned to normal. Darkness descended. On Sunday morning Laura Gilks noticed Frederick Hayball carrying buckets of water back-and-forth from the communal pump in the courtyard. She thought this unusual, since Hayball was extremely lazy and had never been known to help his wife with the domestic chores. At 1pm Laura Gilks observed him leave and, except for the crying of children – a common enough soundtrack to life in such a claustrophobic community – a sense of stillness returned to the courtyard once more.

At noon, having not seen Ellen Hayball emerge, Laura Gilks made up her mind to check on the welfare of her neighbour.

After discovering that Ellen was not in the adjoining empty house, she gathered two other neighbours, Mrs Jenkins and Mrs Prankard, and the three women knocked on the door of the Hayball's home. They received no answer and entered warily, calling out Ellen's name. The children were asleep, so Mrs Gilks ventured upstairs and opened the bedroom door. There, on the floorboards of the scantily furnished room, lay a motionless Ellen Hayball. Her clothing and torso were stained red with blood, as was the bed and the floor surrounding her body. A rough piece of blood-soaked sacking half covered the dreadful wounds to her face and head. One ear had been sliced clean off, and Ellen's left eye had been severed from its socket and lay hanging on her cheek. Laura Gilks temporarily froze in fear, before partially regaining her composure. She ran from the house and roused the courtyards, screaming, 'My God! She's murdered!' Within minutes the courtyard was full and P.C. White, who was walking his beat nearby, was summoned. The constable sounded his whistle and other officers soon arrived.

Mrs Gilks, convinced that she knew where Frederick Hayball could be located, told P.C. White, 'I know where to drop my hand on him in a minute.' She then ran from the courtyard to the nearby Cross Guns Public House. Inside she found Hayball standing at the bar, talking to a group of other dockers. It was the May Bank Holiday weekend, the bar was packed with coarse, seafaring drinkers, and the air thick with the stench of shag tobacco. Not wishing to enter, she beckoned Hayball from the doorway, but he ignored her gestures. Emboldened, she walked towards the group of men and pleaded with him,

'Follow me. They have discovered your wife on the bedroom floor, she is dead or dying, come home.'

'Alright,' he replied, 'let me have another glass of beer, and

I'll be home within five minutes of you.'

'Oh, bother the beer,' she retorted, 'come at once, your wife is dead!'

Hayball seemed more concerned that his drinking comrades would ridicule him for being nagged by a women, and pleaded with her, 'Woman, don't let the boys hear you.'

Laura Gilks left the Cross Guns and returned to Jones's Court to inform P.C White of Hayball's whereabouts, convinced that Hayball would be following close behind her.

'He is in the Cross Guns.' she informed P.C. White. The constable, together with another officer, quickly ran to the nearby public house, arriving there less than five minutes after Mrs Gilks had left Hayball there. Nevertheless, when the two officers entered the pub's saloon bar, Hayball's drink sat untouched on the bar. The room was empty and Hayball was nowhere to be seen.

Superintendent Croker was placed in charge of the hunt for Hayball, and he wasted no time in organising a search of the surrounding district. Officers on bicycles were ordered to search the narrow, and tightly packed, streets and alleyways in the area. Although the fugitive had only a few minutes head-start on the authorities, the logistics of a busy port like Bristol often played into the hands of fleeing criminals. It was possible for someone, with even a superficial knowledge of the port, to climb aboard an empty barge or boat, stow away on a departing cargo ship, or even legitimately board their own vessel before the harbour authorities had been notified. Just like the mysterious attacker of the Chinese sailor Fai Kai, in *The Portway Taxi-cab Murder*, or the unknown assassin in *The Odeon Cinema Murder*, the sprawling docks provided an absconding killer with yet another means of escape. Superintendent Croker ordered a search of the numerous cargo vessels docked alongside Bristol Bridge, although several had already put out into the Bristol Channel, perhaps unwittingly carrying an undiscovered stowaway. Streets and alleyways throughout the city were searched, and a description was issued to the local newspapers,

'Frederick William Hayball, whose apprehension is sought for the murder of his wife on 20th May; age about 34, height 5 ft. 9$^{1/2}$ inches, stout build, complexion fresh, hair dark brown, eyes brown, anchor and two dots tattooed on forearm; dress, when last seen, dark coat, patch on one shoulder, moleskin trousers, cap, supposed white muffler with blue spots. A seaman, but has recently worked as a dock labourer. Native of Bristol. May endeavour to get to sea. Information to the Chief Constable, Bristol.'

In the meantime, patrols at the docks kept a sharp lookout for anyone matching the fugitive's description and the river was searched in case he had taken his own life. A body was sighted in the water, however, it proved to be another poor soul, and not Frederick Hayball. Had Hayball drowned himself in the river, his corpse should have floated to the surface within a few days. No body was ever found.

Meanwhile, as the search intensified in Bristol, the story rapidly spread throughout the whole country. Superintendent Croker was forced to issue a statement to the country's newspapers,

'A sharp lookout has been kept out for Hayball. One witness has come forward, who is certain that they saw him crossing the St Philip's Bridge shortly after leaving the Cross Guns beerhouse. At present, however, his whereabouts remain a mystery.'

Meanwhile, an examination of the crime scene revealed a bloody hatchet in the kitchen sink. A concerted attempt had been made by the killer to clean the weapon. This had removed all traces of blood from the blade; nevertheless, the police laboratory was able to detect bloodstains on the splintered and damaged handle of the hatchet, confirming it as the murder weapon. In a rather macabre twist, the killer had also attempted to sharpen the blade, possibly hoping to dismember the body and avoid detection. Most murderers underestimate the strong stomach required for such a brutal act, and Hayball may well have been too squeamish for such an undertaking, and perhaps had hoped to first stiffen his resolve at the Cross Guns Public House, before returning to complete the gruesome task. Or conceivably, a wave of remorse had changed his mind and he instead chose to cover his wife's face with a piece of sacking to lessen the shame of his vile act.

So severe were the wounds suffered by Ellen Hayball that the post-mortem doctor took forty-five minutes to catalogue the complete list of her dreadful injuries. At the resulting coroner's inquest at Bedminster police station, it was noted that it, 'was most probable the first blow stunned her, if indeed, it did not kill her outright. When dead she was pulled out of bed and laid upon the floor.'

The Bristol coroner, Mr A.E. Barker, asked Ellen's sister, Minnie, 'Do you know anything of the circumstances leading to your sister's death?'

'It is no more than I expected these last four years. I always made up my mind to hear of it at night, between eleven and twelve, not in the daytime.' she answered.

The inquest jury took less than three minutes to reach a verdict of 'Wilful murder against Frederick William Hayball.'

With the formality of the coroner's inquest over, Ellen was buried on 28th May at the burial ground belonging to Redfield Wesleyan Chapel, located behind Church Road. Her sister, Minnie, her mother, Ann, and friends and neighbours from Jones's Court attended.

The following verse was printed on a memorial card and given to the mourners at the graveside:

Like a flower in bloom cut down in its prime
Leaving her motherless children behind
How wretched her life quickly it passed
She clung to her husband until the last
Like a bird with its wings he very soon fled
Leaving the poor creature on the floor quite dead
How sweet to rest upon that shore
When pain and sorrow are no more

Although a record still exists of Ellen's burial, recorded as 'No. 3498, May 28th, Ellen Scudder Milsom Hayball, Coroner's orders', it is no longer possible to visit her grave. The site of the cemetery was flattened during the 1970s and now lies a metre-and-a-half underneath the City Academy Sports Ground. It is thought that more than 3,000 undisturbed graves remain there.

The Wesleyan Chapel itself was finally sold in 1979 and is now the Sanatan Deevya Mandal Bristol Hindu Temple. It was founded by members of the Hindu community who had fled from Uganda in the early 1970s.

Returning to the events of 1899, the investigation continued. Although the police were now certain that Hayball had brutally murdered his wife, and his description had been widely circulated, there was still no sign of the fugitive. Had he taken his own life, or was he hiding somewhere close by? Hayball had been brought up in Sussex Street, near to St Philip's railway station, and had worked in or around the docks for most of his adult life. Possibly he had been able to evade detection, possibly hidden on a goods train leaving from St Philips's or Temple Meads railway stations. Yet there were no reported sightings at any freight depot or station

anywhere in the country. Perhaps, Superintendent Croker surmised, Hayball had not left Bristol at all. After all, he knew the area well and had many drinking associates and criminal contacts he had met during his stints in prison. Someone in the city could be hiding him.

As word spread outward from Bristol, there were reported sightings of Hayball in Bath, Plymouth, Cardiff, and even as far away as Canada, however these all proved to be red herrings. Gradually, as the weeks passed, Superintendent Croker felt that Hayball had somehow managed, in the few minutes between his discovery in the Cross Guns by Mrs Gilks and the arrival of the police, to successfully hide himself somewhere in the vicinity of Bristol docks; and then managed to either stowaway or legitimately board a ship. Officers were despatched to the Alexandria Docks in Newport, the Tawe Basin in Swansea, and the vast Cardiff Bay Docks complex, to watch for any ships arriving from Bristol. However, no one matching Hayball's description was spotted. Speculation rose that he had may have secreted himself on a vessel bound for more distant ports. But crucially, the police had no idea on which ship, or to what destination, their elusive fugitive might be heading.

THE TEMPLE MURDER (PART TWO)

Time passed, and by mid-August 1899 the manhunt for Frederick Hayball was proving to be a fruitless one. Detectives began to consider the possibility that their fugitive had managed to board a vessel, destined for some distant port, either immediately, or within a few days of murdering his wife. The most likely escape route for the wanted man seems to have been on the eastbound trade routes, probably steaming to San Francisco, via Australia (a voyage he had previously undertaken); conceivably onboard a vessel on which he had formerly served. Unfortunately, in 1899, once a ship had reached the open seas, no radio signal from land was possible. Marconi's first transatlantic wireless transmission was still two years away, and reliable ship-to-shore radio communication – over anything but a short distance – further still. Nevertheless, all hope of detaining the guilty man before he could disappear among the thousands of other arrivals in San Francisco, was not lost.

If a faster ship, bound for Ellis Island in New York, could convey a message to the authorities there, it would still be possible for the New York Police to cable a telegram via the American transcontinental telegraph network to the west coast, before any ship circumnavigating the longer, eastbound, trade route to San Francisco had docked.

Bristol detectives then set about the task of narrowing down a list of possible ships on which Frederick Hayball may have embarked. In the seven days immediately following his disappearance and the murder of his wife, eight vessels were identified on which Hayball might have conceivably escaped. The British ship *Duchalburn,* which had sailed from London four days after the murder, and was now eight-nine days out at sea. The *Beacon Rock*, eighty-eight days out from the capital. Three departures from Swansea Docks were also considered possible escape routes for Hayball. The British ship *Glenbreck*, which had left Swansea ninety days earlier, along with three French barks, the *Sainte Annie, Cambronne*, and *Genevieve Mollinos.* Two further British vessels sailings for San Francisco from Cardiff were also regarded as potential safe passages for Hayball; the *Dunsdale*, and the *Inversnauld*, eighty-two days and eighty-six days at sea respectively.

The crew manifests for each ship were scrutinised for anyone boarding under the name of 'Hayball', although Superintendent Croker realised it was a relatively simple task in 1899 for a sailor to sign on as a crewmember at the last minute, and under a false name. No identification papers or visas were required to enter the USA and passports did not become a necessity until the outbreak of the Great War. When, and if, Hayball's ship finally docked at the Port of San Francisco, and assuming he was travelling under a false name, an extremely accurate description and picture would be needed to detain him.

The description previously issued to the British newspapers was despatched via message and then telegraph to veteran Chief of Police Isaish Lees in San Francisco. Accompanying the description was a specially created artist's impression, using the latest technical advances in printing plate transfer, which enabled a remarkable – almost photograph like – reproduction of Hayball's image to be printed in the *San Francisco Call and Post* newspaper. A full decade before the wireless telegraph system was famously used to apprehend Dr Crippen, the Bristol and San Francisco police forces were at the forefront of crime detection.

Chief of Police Lees issued the description and image to the *Call and Post,* then placed his two most reliable officers, Sergeant Steve Bunner and Officer W. Fergusson, at Meiggs Wharf to apprehend Hayball as his ship arrived. The two men were stationed at the port for an entire month and boarded all eight vessels, on which Hayball was thought to be aboard, as they arrived. However, they were unable to find anyone matching the fugitive's description. Although an arrest was reported in the British newspapers, this proved to be erroneous. If Hayball had been onboard one of those eight ships, he somehow managed to avoid detection. Ultimately, with their resources stretched by a corruption scandal and a number of other high-profile cases, the San Francisco line of enquiry was scaled down. Frederick Hayball seemed to have once again escaped the long arms of the law.

As the new century dawned, the murder appears to have largely slipped from the public consciousness. As Britain entered the Edwardian era – often referred to as 'The Golden Age of Crime' – those with an appetite for sensational murder stories were amply entertained. Hayball's 'Wanted' description did not reappear in the newspapers for almost three years. However, the search for the wanted man burst into life again on 20th April 1902, when Bristol police received a telegram from their Cardiff counterparts informing them that a man in their custody strongly matched the description of Frederick Hayball. Detective-Sergeant Churchill, who had worked on the investigation in 1899 and knew Hayball by sight, took the 3:10pm train to Cardiff in high spirits. It seemed certain that the police had finally caught their man. Regrettably, it proved to be yet another false lead in the frustrating quest for the wanted man. The prisoner, although he bore a striking facial resemblance to Hayball, was six feet in height and proved to be an Irish-American labourer employed at Cardiff docks. Detective-Sergeant Churchill realised the mistake instantly, and ordered that the man be set free at once. Before returning empty-handed to Bristol, Churchill apologised profusely and bought the aggrieved man a drink in a nearby public house.

Once again it seemed that Frederick Hayball had escaped justice. Another two years would pass, until the Bristol police again received a telegram from another constabulary, stating confidently that they had arrested 'The Temple Murderer'. This time, the man had admitted to being Frederick William Hayball and to murdering his wife in Bristol five years earlier with a hatchet. According to the information wired to Bristol by Salford police, they had taken a 'seafaring Bristolian' into custody on a charge of passing a counterfeit banknote. After initially giving his name as 'Harford', the man had subsequently admitted to being Hayball, and to having fled to America in 1899, before returning to England in March 1904. Once again, Detective-Sergeant Churchill was sent north by train, this time to arrest Hayball in Salford and charge him with murder. The national newspapers printed the story with much excitement as speculation mounted. However, yet again, despite the prisoner's confession, Churchill was to be disappointed. The man was not Hayball, but a petty criminal from Bristol called John Morgan who had actually spent the previous five years, not in America, but in a Manchester jail. He had been familiar with the Hayball case after reading about it in the Bristol newspapers. Morgan was given a further six-month sentence for passing forged banknotes, and Churchill returned to Bristol empty-handed. Why John Morgan claimed to be Frederick Hayball is not known. Perhaps he desired his fifteen minutes of fame, maybe he was forced to confess to the murder by over-zealous detectives, or conceivably, he had found life on the 'outside' too difficult and wished to return to prison. Whatever the answer, it has become just one part of the perplexing mystery regarding the disappearance of Frederick Hayball.

There were no more reported sightings of the wanted man. He seems to have simply disappeared.

This leaves an intriguing question. What happened to the elusive 'Temple Murderer'? There are five tantalising possibilities.

Firstly, in a fit of remorse and shame, he took his own life shortly after fleeing the crime scene. However, this appears to be the least likely eventuality, since no body was ever discovered, and the act seems sorely out of character for such a violent and hot-headed man.

Secondly, Hayball managed to successfully board a ship not bound for San Francisco, either unobserved or as crewmember travelling under a false name. He was then able to disembark at a distant port undetected, enabling him to melt away into the crowds and begin a new life under his new alias.

Although most observers have concluded that one of these two outcomes is the most likely, during the research for this story, I have uncovered three further potential solutions to the riddle, not previously known. Firstly, the little-known story of the *Beacon Rock*.

One of the vessels originally highlighted as potentially carrying Hayball to San Francisco, the *Beacon Rock*, docked at Meiggs Wharf on schedule and was duly met by detectives Bunner and Ferguson of the City Police. All passengers and crew were accounted for, with the exception of one sailor, Enoch Oleman. Oleman had complained of feeling seriously ill just prior to docking, and had been taken from the *Beacon*

Rock by special launch (before the ship's passengers and crew had disembarked) and then admitted into hospital in San Francisco. Once there, Oleman informed doctors that he was suffering from the effects of scurvy (caused by a serious vitamin C deficiency, created by a lack of fruit, vegetables, and fresh food in the diet. Untreated, scurvy can lead to bleeding gums, loosened teeth and bleeding under the skin). Oleman complained that the *Beacon Rock*'s onboard supply of beef, flour, and drinking water had been unfit for human consumption, resulting in his illness. A full investigation was carried out at the request of the British Consul General in San Francisco (an outbreak of scurvy on a British ship was considered a serious matter). However, no signs of the disease were located onboard, no other crewmembers complained, and the food supply was found to be more than adequate. The matter was even raised in parliament, due to the reputation of the British maritime industry. Oleman was assumed to have been either a malingerer, or suffering from 'a general debility.' He promptly discharged himself and was never seen again. Furthermore, there is no record of anyone of that name ever boarding a ship from the UK, or being born, living, or dying in either the UK or the United States. Was this mysterious sailor really Frederick Hayball. We will probably never know.

The next theory also involves the *Beacon Rock*. Perhaps Hayball, realising that San Francisco police were waiting to question all crewmembers as the vessel weighed anchor, merely hid himself on board and waited for the ship to depart again, hoping possibly to disembark unnoticed elsewhere? Although the authorities at all scheduled stopping points on the *Beacon Rock*'s voyage had been warned that a fugitive from the UK may be on board, an unscheduled stop might have presented Hayball with an opportunity for escape. After leaving the Port of San Francisco, the *Beacon Rock* continued its round the world journey, finally arriving at Port Pirie in eastern Australia during September 1900. A year-long voyage across the South Seas, thousands of miles from home, would have certainly fitted the needs of a man seeking to escape from the Bristol police. The ship was then scheduled to dock in Wellington, New Zealand, on 4th October, which may have been Hayball's intended final destination – as far away from British justice as possible.

However, the *Beacon Rock* failed to arrive in Wellington on 4th October. Days gradually turned into weeks, yet still the ship failed to materialise. No other docking vessels reported sighting the missing craft at sea, although several ships had recorded severe storms in their ships' logs. Weeks slowly turned into months; but with no effective way of locating or communicating with the missing vessel, she was finally presumed to be lost at sea. If Hayball had indeed been on board the *Beacon Rock*, that might have been a fitting end to his unsavoury story. Nevertheless, there was to be one more twist in the tale.

In January 1901, reports reached the *Auckland Star* newspaper that the badly damaged *Beacon Rock* had made land at Concepción in south-central Chile, almost 6,000 miles away. The ship had nearly capsized, after being battered by severe storms and winds, which had rendered its rudder useless and badly damaged the haul. After drifting aimlessly eastward for three months, pounded by colossal sea swells and shipping water alarmingly, the vessel eventually sighted land and limped to shore in South America. Had Hayball been on board and survived this horrendous journey, he may have taken employment at the docks or among the large British community in Concepción, successfully managing to keep his true identity secret.

With no further sightings of Hayball ever reported, either

in the UK or elsewhere, perhaps he really did manage to evade British justice and carve a new life for himself in some distant corner of the world. And there the story would seem to end, until my research led me to this lost and forgotten letter and story, pieced together in 1953 by the *Bristol Evening Post*.

Albert Flay, then aged nineteen, had witnessed Hayball enter Jones's Court on the day of his wife's death in 1899. The seventy-three-year-old Bristolian later became convinced he had met Hayball in the years following the murder. An *Evening Post* reporter interviewed Mr Flay, following receipt of his letter, and put together the following story, which includes portions of Albert Flay's original letter;

> Whit-Sunday of 1899 was a peaceful day with little to disturb the tranquil early summer atmosphere. To 19-year-old Mr Flay it was far too quiet. As he wandered slowly down Victoria Street in the Temple district his thoughts were broken by a woman's scream. He looked across the road where an arch led into a cul-de-sac A woman suddenly appeared in the arch, "Police! Fetch the police!" she shrieked "There's been a murder."
>
> Policeman went to look for the husband and discovered him in a nearby public house, The Cross Guns. Although officers raced to the public house just a few minutes later, the time lag had been sufficient for Hayball to disappear. An immediate search of the area proved fruitless. In the days that followed, news of the increasing efforts by the police to catch Hayball made headlines. But they never succeeded. The following year the Boer War broke out and Mr Flay volunteered. Taken with enteric fever, he was sent to a military hospital in South Africa.
>
> "The patients were a mixed lot," Mr Flay recalled,

"but one man with large side-whiskers caught my attention. Seeing that he was being watched, the man moved across the room and said hello to me. In the conversation that followed the man said he was by trade a ship's carpenter, but had become a medical orderly as the pay was better. He spoke with a pronounced Bristol accent and, as the conversation continued, I became increasingly suspicious.

"What part of Bristol are you from?" I asked. The man did not reply.

"Are you the man who killed his wife – Mr Hayball?" I enquired.

"You want to know too much," replied the man, and hurriedly switched to another topic.

Shortly afterwards I was moved from the hospital to a convalescent home. As I was leaving the hospital the stranger called out to me, "By God's will, we shall meet again."

And meet again we did. Two months passed and I was bound for the Transvaal having recovered from illness. Nearing a rail junction, the train in which I was travelling pulled to a standstill and a few minutes later another train drew alongside. I looked out of the window and imagine my surprise when I saw the same man with the side whiskers leaning out of the carriage opposite. He waved to me and called out, 'I told you we would meet again.' A few minutes later his train moved off and it was a long time before I was destined to see him for the last time."

The Great War had ended and Mr Flay returned to Bristol, where it became a habit for him to call at an hotel in Cheltenham Road. One day after parking his horse and gig he entered the saloon bar. From the adjacent taproom he could hear a man talking in a loud voice.

"I heard the barman tell him to drink up and leave,"

recalled Mr Flay, "when the man spoke again I realised I knew the voice. I moved across to see into the taproom. He was standing at the bar and was dressed like a tramp. Recognising him as the man I had seen in hospital in South Africa, and then in the train, I felt like speaking to him, but he was so shabbily dressed I didn't wish to be seen with him. And so, as I passed him on the way out, I merely said 'Hello' to him. He followed me outside, terribly excited and kept saying it was God's wish that we should have met again. He then asked me to leave this 'Godforsaken country' with him, and said he had plenty of money, pulling out of his torn pocket a bag of golden sovereigns to prove it. But we had very little to talk about really and, to get rid of him, I said I would sell my turn-out and meet him at six o'clock, when I would go off with him on road. I never returned and I never saw him again."

That it was Frederick Hayball he met on all three occasions, Mr Flay claims he has no doubt. But as he points out: "At no point did he admit to being the wanted man, and I had no actual proof that he was – only a strong personal belief."

Hayball was 37 when the murder was committed and if he were alive today, he would be 91.

(*Bristol Evening Post* Special Reporter 1953)

Did Albert Flay really meet Frederick Hayball three times? If this letter and article from 1953 is to be believed, he did.

While it is unlikely that definite proof of Hayball's fate will ever be established, it is almost certain that he lived out the remainder of his life in as much abject squalor, fear, and misery as the short existence he inflicted on his poor wife.

THE DEVIL IN CLIFTON WOOD

Saturday 25th May 1907 was a warm and pleasant early summer's day in Bristol. Police Constable Mead was on duty in Clifton, at the junction of Regent Street and Royal York Crescent. He looked at his pocket-watch, it was 12:20pm. As he did so, a haggard and anxious middle-aged man approached him.

The man spoke first, 'I have murdered my wife, Mary. I thought I should tell you before I jump over the bridge.'

P.C. Mead was taken aback, but from the man's distressed demeanour, and the blood on his waistcoat, he instantly realised the gravity of the situation. The constable also knew the nearby Clifton Suspension Bridge, although only open for forty years, had already claimed the lives of scores of anguished souls.

Mead engaged the man in conversation, and noticed that he was trembling although the day was warm, 'What is your name?' he asked.

'James Gibson, sir.', the man replied, 'you had better come with me to the house.'

Gibson led the police constable along Lower Clifton Hill, then past the villas in Clifton Wood Road, until they reached Southernhay Avenue, a narrow cul-de-sac of terraced cottages which sloped down towards Brandon Hill in the distance. As they approached number ten on the left and walked up the steps to the front door, P.C. Mead instinctively gripped his right hand around the leather strap of his wooden 'life preserver'. He did not know what to expect when they entered the house.

On entering the narrow passageway, they made their way through to the dimly lit kitchen at the rear. There, slumped in a bloodstained chair in the centre of the room, P.C. Mead found the lifeless body of Mary Gibson. Her throat had been cut with such force that her head had been all but sliced from her body, revealing a gaping wound. The bones of her upper neck were visible, and the woman's clothes were stained a dark crimson. Mary's face and head were blackened and distorted and there appeared to be heavy trauma to the skull.

'What did you use to do this?' P.C. Mead asked in disbelief.

Gibson pointed to a bloodstained cut-throat razor and knife lying on the kitchen table, then added, 'I finished her off with the flat iron.' He gestured towards the heavy iron which now lay, matted in blood and hair, on the floor beside the chair.

Mead summoned Dr Martin and two other constables. James Gibson was then arrested and taken to Brandon Hill Police Station.

Following an inquest at Bridewell Police Court, at which a verdict of 'Wilful murder' was recorded in the death of Mary Ann Gibson, James Gibson was remanded at the lunatic wing of Horfield Prison for observation, and a date was set for his trial.

James Gibson finally stood trial in Bristol for the murder of his wife a month later, on 28th June. After being assisted into the dock by a police officer, he stood quietly and listened intently to Mr Justice Bray.

'Prisoner at the bar, you are charged that you did feloniously, wilfully, and with malice aforethought, kill and murder Mary Ann Gibson, at Bristol on the 25th May, 1907. How do you plead?'

Through his barrister, Mr Thomas Inskip K.C., Gibson entered a plea of 'Not guilty due to grounds of insanity.'

The accused man, although aged only fifty-eight, appeared far older. He had previously served for twenty-one years in the Royal Engineers, including a substantial period overseas during various colonial uprisings. Gibson had then been given an honourable discharge and full army pension. Since retiring, he had not returned to his native Scotland, instead taking employment as a 'wheel-chairman' in Bristol (a now largely forgotten occupation, in which wealthy and often invalided ladies were transported around the streets of Bristol, Bath, and Cheltenham, on rickshaw-like chairs. The 'wheel-chairmen' were licensed by the city and became a familiar sight in the era before the motorcar dominated our roads).

Gibson and his wife moved to Southernhay Avenue in Clifton Wood following his army discharge, however the marriage had not been a happy one, as prosecuting barrister Raymond Asquith K.C. noted, 'The man and wife had been intemperate in their habits of late. Mrs Gibson especially so. Mrs Gibson was known to the neighbours as "Mrs. Catastrophe", as she was always so full of her troubles. James Gibson, who was a well-known character in Clifton, was one of the wheel-chairmen, and was looked upon as a particularly civil individual. You will hear evidence later from the couple's daughter, that when she called on them last Sunday, and wished her parents goodnight, Gibson replied. "Goodnight, if we are not both dead before you see us again".'

'The circumstances surrounding the case,' Asquith continued in his address to the jury, 'prove it to be one of those domestic tragedies which we frequently come across in the course of our profession. The case is not devoid of difficulty, but when you have heard the evidence, and under the direction of the learned judge, you will be in a position to say whether there are any circumstances surrounding it, which would justify you in bringing in a verdict which will reduce the offence to one of a lesser degree than that with which he is now charged. You will also hear evidence from certain doctors who will be able to say if the circumstances and conditions of this man's life and health will warrant you in relieving him from the responsibility which his act had occasioned.'

Raymond Asquith K.C., although still only twenty-nine years of age, had already risen to the bar and earned the respect of his colleagues and peers. He was a distinguished Oxford scholar, a poet, a member of the fashionable group of intellectuals and aristocrats known as 'The Coterie', and the eldest son of soon-to-be Prime Minister Herbert H. Asquith.

Having ensured the jurors' attention, Raymond Asquith began the Crown's case against Gibson,

'Members of the jury, evidence will be given as to the frequent quarrels between the couple. Upon the day in question which, according to Mr Gibson's statement, he took the life of his wife, the last time that she was seen alive was about twenty minutes past eleven in the morning. At that hour she was spoken to by a neighbour, Mrs Jukes, who had a conversation with her which lasted ten minutes. Mrs Jukes remembered that Mrs Gibson was in a calm mood, and not in any way quarrelsome.

After Mrs Gibson departed, Mrs Jukes did not hear any quarrelling between Mr and Mrs Gibson, coming from the house next-door.

Members of the jury, I beg you to keep that fact in mind, because if it can be proved that this crime was committed in the heat of passion, and under provocation from his wife, it might be that you would be justified in reducing the nature of the offence.'

The Crown appeared to be offering the jury a simple and straightforward conclusion to the case. Asquith continued, 'In any case, we know that at twenty minutes past eleven the deceased woman was calm and collected when she entered the house. Mrs Jukes did not see the accused from that moment on, and the next link we have in the chain of events connected with the crime came about midday, when the accused man called in at the Portland Vaults, in Portland Street, where he had two penny worth of whisky. The barmaid who served him said that the man was then calm in his demeanour, even though his visit to the Portland Vaults must have been immediately after the murder had been committed. As the barmaid is well acquainted with the man, that matter is an important one. When he left Portland Street he made his way to Regent Street, and about twenty past twelve he approached P.C. Mead, and said, "I have murdered my wife; I had better tell you before I jump over the bridge." It was upon this confession that the accused man was then charged. This confession that he had murdered his wife was corroborated by the fact that upon the constable taking him to his house he found his wife sitting in a chair with her throat cut and with an injury to her head.

It is important that you also remember that, with regard to the prisoner's statement that he would jump over the bridge, a Bristol jury will probably know the locality and have little doubt that he meant the Suspension Bridge, from which so many unfortunate people have taken their lives. Yet, despite his claim of insanity, this man had sufficient control over himself to go to a policeman and tell him what he had done, then lead that policeman back to his home, and to point out the weapons used.

Referring to the killing itself, so deep was the cut inflicted in this woman's throat, that her vertebra was gashed. Our evidence will show that a very determined murder was committed.

The jury must also bear in mind what I have already pointed out – that, so far as we are aware, there was no quarrel before the perpetration of the deed. In fact, nothing was said about any quarrel having preceded the crime until some three weeks afterwards, and only when the prisoner alluded to it in conversation with one of the doctors at the lunatic asylum. In the same way, nothing was said, till some time had elapsed, about the state of the prisoner's health. By instructions from the Town Clerk, who had charge of the prosecution, the prisoner had been kept under careful observation, and one report, furnished on June 8th, led to another being made on June 16th; while a third was furnished by a physician of the lunatic asylum on June 21st. These reports have been placed in the hands of those engaged in the defence of the accused man, for them to deal with as they deem wise.'

After finishing his lengthy address, Asquith called P.C. Mead to the stand.

'P.C. Mead, you accompanied the prisoner back to his home. What did he do when you entered the kitchen?', Asquith enquired.

'He pointed to the cut-throat razor and a knife, which were lying on the table. They were bloodstained and the razor was open.'

At this point, Thomas Inskip K.C. was granted the opportunity to cross-examine the witness on behalf of the defence;

'P.C. Mead, did the prisoner give you the impression that he was not only strange in his manner, but was also demented?'

'He was certainly very strange in his manner, sir.'

'Out of his mind?'

'I should think so, sir, from the appearance of him.'

Mrs Martha Jukes, the Gibson's next-door neighbour, was also cross-examined by Thomas Inskip, 'Mrs Jukes, how was Mrs Gibson when you spoke to her on the morning of her death?'

'Well, we had a conversation, but she was normal. She was sober that morning.'

'And had you heard Mrs Gibson and her husband arguing that day?'

'No, sir. I last heard them quarrelling in Easter week, but not after that.'

'Would you say Mrs Gibson was an excitable woman?'

'Yes.'

'Thank you. No further questions.'

Miss Hollis, the barmaid at the Portland Vaults was also cross-examined by Mr Inskip as he attempted to show a degree of mitigation to account for the accused man's behaviour, 'Did you serve Mr Gibson with drink on the day of his wife's death, Miss Hollis?'

'Yes. I gave him two-penny worth of whisky about twelve o'clock. I spoke to him. I noticed nothing unusual about his manner. He always seemed a harmless, inoffensive man. I think he was sober.'

At this juncture, Mr Asquith interjected for the prosecution, 'How did you know he was not drunk, Miss Hollis?'

'I have occasionally seen him under the influence of drink, but not often. I do not think he was on that day.'

Next came the medical evidence from Dr Robert Martin, the Clifton doctor who had been summoned on the day of the murder.

'Your honour, I was called to the house in Southernhay Avenue and found the woman with her throat cut from ear to ear. The wound was so deep that it extended to the vertebrae at the back of the neck, which was visible. Two of the upper Cervical bones had a notch on them from the blade of a knife. It is not possible to determine whether the blow from the flatiron was administered first, however, it was delivered with some force, and all the wounds were certainly of a very determined nature.'

No doubt anticipating any resulting questions from the two opposing barristers, Dr Martin added, 'The wounds may certainly have been inflicted by someone with an unreasoning mind, nevertheless, they may have also been caused by a man in a state of paroxysm.'

It was now time for the Crown to rest and Thomas Inskip to begin the case for the defence.

'Call Margaret Annie Gibson.'

The accused man's tearful daughter was escorted to the witness stand and asked to explain the relationship between her parents,

'My mother was fifty-seven years old. She and my father

had not been happy. They frequently quarrelled, as my mother's mode of life caused my father much unhappiness. She was in the habit of drinking more than was good for her, and was constantly in a drunken condition. Both my mother and father were fined for drunkenness in 1904.'

'And was she violent towards your father when in that state?', ventured Mr Inskip.

'Yes, and at other times too. I have seen her attack my father with all manner of things and order him to leave the house.'

'What sort of things, Miss Gibson?'

'All sorts of things. A poker, a cup, a plate. Anything she could get hold of. He generally tried to keep out of her way on these occasions. But he was generally forbearing and patient towards her. Latterly, since Whitsuntide, he has seemed very depressed. I saw him the night before the occurrence and he was very strange. He complained to me of pains in his head.'

A more complete picture of James Gibson's gloomy existence was added by his younger brother, Alexander,

'I frequently visited my brother, who had a miserable home. I suggested to him that he should have a separation, but he thought it was his duty to live with his wife as long as he could.'

'And what about in more recent times, Mr Gibson?'

'In recent times, my brother has appeared worried and depressed. I thought he was losing his willpower. I saw him only yesterday, at Horfield Prison. My brother told me that just before poor Mary was killed, someone whispered in his ear, "Do it, do it, do it." He also said he could feel the devil sitting by his left ankle.'

The defence then called Henry Lewis Morgan, a retired civil servant, to the witness box.

'Your honour,' Mr Morgan began, 'I was formerly

engaged at Tudor Hall, the military establishment in Clifton, where the accused man was also employed. He had furnished married quarters on the premises, and up to1883 he appeared to live very comfortably with his wife. Then a change came, due to the wife contracting drinking habits. From that period onwards, the whole course of his life seemed to be altered.'

Dr Lionel Weatherly was then asked to testify to James Gibson's mental state;

'Your honour, I have had thirty-three years' experience in the treatment of nervous diseases. I examined the prisoner at Horfield Prison and found him to be a man above ordinary intelligence, though distinctly neurotic. The prisoner has suffered from asthma, which is a disease of the nerves, for many years. He told me that he had drunk a good deal of late, his wife being a terrible woman to live with.

In the weeks before his wife's death he had suffered from hallucinations, both of hearing and of sight. Apparently, a voice or voices spoke to him through his left ear. Sometimes he would hear his name called when he was in the street. Sometimes other things were said to him, apparently through his left ear, which he did not appear to understand. For a day or two before the murder a voice persistently repeated the words, " Do it, do it, do it." When I asked him to explain, he replied, "I do not know what it means."

With regard to his hallucinations of sight, these seem to have been equally significant. He said he had seen a blood-red mark on his left ankle, and he believed the devil had entered into him through that red mark. He had seen a figure which must have been the devil or one of his imps coming out of this mark, and he believed that was how the devil took possession of him.

When looking through a window, the glass would appear blood red to him, with an image of the devil looking back at him.'

'Thank you, doctor, and what did the patient tell you of the woman's death?' Thomas Inskip asked.

'He said he had a few words with his wife the night before, and when he went to bed he spent a restless night, constantly hearing the voice or voices repeating the words, "Do it, do it, do it." After breakfast, on the day of her death, his wife went to wash the things used at the meal, but some time afterwards he found that she had still not finished the work. They came to words in consequence and his wife approached him in a threatening way. She jumped at his throat, and then fell back into a chair. While she was there, he cut her throat, and then hit her on the head with the flatiron. He could not say why he had used each terrible violence; all he could explain was that the voice kept saying, "Do it; do it."

From my experience of people who have suffered hallucinations, they frequently feel compelled to commit acts, over which they have no control. In my opinion, his mind is absolutely obsessed with the commands given by the voice he hears.'

'And have you experienced anything like this before, doctor?'

'Yes. It is common. I have myself been attacked by patients who had before been most friendly with me, and who, five minutes afterwards, have been most friendly again. They say they felt bound to do it. I believe that during such obsessions, a man's willpower is quite beyond his control.

The prisoner told me he had often left home with the intention of killing himself, and had once taken a rope to the Downs to hang himself, but his heart always failed him. After killing his wife, he said he went to the Portland Street Vaults to have some whisky, thinking it might wake him up sufficiently to allow him to throw himself over the Bridge, but he found he could not do it, so he gave himself up to the police instead.'

'And what is your conclusion please, doctor, to this man's mental condition?'

'While I cannot certify the prisoner as insane, I equally could not certify him as sane. Five members of his family have all exhibited signs of mental deficiency. I can only suggest that the prisoner acted under the command of the voice he fancied he heard, and did not know that he was doing wrong.'

Mr Justice Bray thanked Dr Weatherley, before issuing his final summation to the jury,

'Members of the jury, I consider that you would be justified, upon the evidence before you in this case, in saying that the prisoner is not of sound mind, at the time be committed the deed. If you are of that opinion, they must find him guilty of the offence with which he was charged, but add that he was insane at the time.'

The jury duly retired, but required only three minutes' deliberation, before finding James Gibson 'Guilty of murder, but being of unsound mind.'

The judge ordered that Gibson 'was to be detained in Horfield Prison Lunatic wing during his Majesty's pleasure.'

There are, of course, no winners in such a troubling and poignant case. The tall and distinguished Raymond Asquith K.C., whose personality was usually a rather cold and aloof one, found the case a deeply troubling one. Following yet another unsatisfactory resolution to a trial a few months later, he recorded in a private letter,

'Every day I hate my profession more and wish more that I were rich.'

His brilliant career was to be cut sadly short. At the outbreak of the Great War, he was commissioned as a second lieutenant in the Queen's Westminster Rifles. After transferring to the Grenadier Guards he requested a frontline assignment, a request which was reluctantly granted just before the Battle of the Somme. On 15th September 1916 he was shot in the chest during an assault on German-held Ginchy (previously called Guinchy) in Northern France. He casually lit a cigarette to hide the seriousness of his injuries from his platoon, so that the attack could continue. Raymond Asquith died whilst being carried back to a casualty clearing station behind the British lines.

His father, by then the Prime Minister, was informed at Downing Street. Winston Churchill later wrote a poignant memorial which was published in *The Times*,

'When the Grenadiers strode into the crash and thunder of the Somme, he went to his fate cool, poised, resolute, matter of fact, debonair. And well we know that his father, then bearing the supreme burden of the State, would proudly have marched at his side.'

James Gibson remained in Horfield Prison for the rest of his unhappy life – just a few more short years. His daughter Margaret, who was twenty-seven at time of her mother's death and father's trial, remained in the west country for the rest of her life, eventually passing away in Weston-Super-Mare in 1960 at the age of eighty.

It is not known if she ever visited her father.

THE FARMYARD BOMBER

On the morning of Monday 9th April 1984, Bristolians woke to a shocking and explosive news story that, quite literally, blew the fifty-sixth Academy Awards off the front pages.

The drama unfolded at Widden Hill Farm, a quiet dairy farm in the hamlet of Horton, close to Yate on the outskirts of Bristol. Farmer's wife Maggie Backhouse climbed into the family's X-registration Volvo estate for her morning trip to pick up some supplies from the local vet in Wotton-under-Edge. It was a journey she had undertaken many times. As Maggie turned the key in the ignition a crudely built, but lethal, car bomb exploded. The device had been constructed from two parallel sections of metal pipe, threaded with a detonator and wired together. Gunpowder from twelve shotgun shells had been meticulously placed inside as an explosive charge. Sickeningly, the metal pipes had then been packed with some 4,000 lead pellets, purposefully intended to cause the maximum amount of injury. Finally, the bomb had been wired through the ignition and carefully placed underneath the driver's seat, with the force of the explosion designed to travel upwards, through the car seat, killing the victim instantly.

Miraculously, the blast did not kill thirty-seven-year-old Maggie Backhouse, although she suffered severe injuries to her back, buttocks, and legs. She was able to crawl from the car, and was seen by two passers-by. They ran to fetch her husband, forty-four-year-old dairy farmer, Graham

Backhouse, who was working nearby at the time. He had been out of sight, working elsewhere on the farm, and was not immediately aware of exactly what had happened. He rushed to her side and, acting quickly, he telephoned the emergency services, saying, 'My wife has been injured in an explosion.'

It was now 8:20am.

Maggie was rushed to Frenchay Hospital in Bristol, while Graham Backhouse remained at Widden Hill Farm waiting for officers from Avon and Somerset C.I.D. to arrive at the scene.

In 1984 the authorities maintained a high level of alert, following a series of bombing by the IRA at high profile targets such as Oxford Street, the Grand Hotel in Brighton, and the assassinations of Airey Neave MP and Lord Mountbatten. Detectives initial suspicions pointed towards a terrorist link. The Backhouse's neighbour at the time was a retired army officer, perhaps he had been the intended target?

However, investigators quickly changed their minds following a conversation with Graham Backhouse. He informed detectives that for the past few weeks he had been the victim of a campaign of anonymous hate mail and malicious phone calls. Perhaps, police officers now conjectured, Graham Backhouse had been the intended target and not his wife. Backhouse also explained that an unidentified man had claimed that Backhouse had been involved in an affair with his wife, and 'ruined her'. This unknown man even blamed Backhouse for his son's suicide a year earlier.

Graham Backhouse handed the police a note he had found a few days earlier, attached to a severed lamb's head impaled on a fence post at Widden Hill Farm. The note simply read 'You next'.

On the morning of the bombing, according to Backhouse, he had received another anonymous handwritten note, which had been hastily printed in capitals, and included one spelling error,

'Came tyce (sic) last week but the pigs were about. See you soon.'

Backhouse initially told detectives that he believed a neighbour named David Hodkinson was behind the threats, citing his affair with Hodkinson's wife as a motive. However, Hodkinson had been away from the area working, and was quickly eliminated as a suspect.

Margaret Backhouse was kept under twenty-four-hour armed guard, as she lay seriously ill in Frenchay Hospital. Surgeons battled to remove hundreds of lead shot and other metal fragments from deep wounds to her thighs and buttocks. Graham Backhouse was also given an armed police guard at Widden Hill Farm. Police officers were taking no chances. They had no idea who the bomber was, or if he would strike again.

The *Bristol Evening Post* reported the sensational developments;

'A village vendetta led to farmer's wife Mrs Maggie

Backhouse being injured in a car bomb explosion at her home in Horton, near Bristol, today. She was taken to Frenchay Hospital where she was undergoing surgery this afternoon.'

Detective Superintendent Tom Evans, who led the enquiry, briefed the waiting reporters:

'The farm was immediately cordoned off and sniffer dogs are now being used to scour the area. There has been a recent history of anonymous threatening phone calls to the family. We are also investigating a lamb's head, found with a message inside it, which gives us reason to connect it with the telephone calls.'

Meanwhile, detectives and forensic officers continued their exhaustive examination of the crime scene at the farm.

Nine days after the bombing Graham Backhouse insisted that the twenty-four police protection be removed from the farm. He informed detectives that he had installed an alarm system, which he requested be linked directly to the nearest police station at Chipping Sodbury (two miles away). The sophisticated alarm incorporated a panic button which would enable local officers to be in attendance within a matter of minutes, should an incident occur. And so, on 18th April, the armed police guard was reassigned elsewhere, and normality returned to Widden Hill Farm. Detective Superintendent Tom Evans had been understandably cautious about withdrawing police protection. However, eleven more days passed peacefully, and the superintendent began to relax. Perhaps the threat was now over. After all, Graham Backhouse had not reported any more threatening calls or letters.

Then, on the evening of Monday 30th April on-duty officers where suddenly triggered into action when the alarm button from Widden Hill Farm was activated.

Police Constable Richard Yeadon was immediately despatched to the scene. He had no idea what to expect, as the sounding of the alarm at the police station had not been followed by an explanatory phone call. On his arrival, all seemed eerily quiet and normal. Yet something had clearly induced the occupant to activate his panic alarm. Despite fearing for their own safety, PC Yeadon entered the farmhouse through the front door which was unlocked. He called out 'Police!' and 'Police! Mr Backhouse?', as he made his way cautiously inside. There was no response to his call. As he entered the dimly lit passageway PC Yeadon noticed the body of a man slumped at the foot of the stairs. Clutched in the man's right hand was a bloody Stanley knife. A recently discharged shotgun lay on the floor nearby, and the unmistakable smell of gunpowder still lingered in the air. As PC Yeadon approached cautiously, it became obvious that the man was dead. However, to his surprise, it was not Graham Backhouse. The victim was older, shorter, and more slightly built than the farmer.

Suddenly PC Yeadon heard a low moaning sound close by. Swivelling around sharply, he later described what he saw:

'I stepped over the body and saw Mr. Backhouse lying in a curled-up position in the entrance to the lounge. He was sobbing.'

Graham Backhouse lay slumped, one side of his face bleeding heavily; his neck, throat and shirt stained a vivid red. He held his bloodstained hand over a huge gapping gash on the left-hand side of his face and there appeared to be a further wound on his chest. The passageway and the lounge were also spattered with blood spots, seeming to indicate that a violent struggle had taken place.

Graham Backhouse explained that his neighbour, Mr Colyn Bedale-Taylor, had come to the house offering to repair some furniture. Sixty-three-year-old Mr Bedale-Taylor had retired early and become the Horton village 'handyman', undertaking many jobs in the community. In fact, on the morning of his shooting, he had just unveiled a bench and noticeboard he had built for the village school. By this juncture, a further six police cars had arrived at Widden Hill Farm in response to the alarm, creating a sensation in the village and causing more wild rumours to spread.

After receiving urgent medical attention to the severe gashes on his face and chest, Backhouse explained the chain of events to the police. According to Backhouse, Colyn Bedale-Taylor had arrived at Widden Hill Farm offering to repair some furniture. However, Backhouse claimed, Bedale-Taylor became infuriated when he was informed that nothing needed repairing. He then accused Backhouse of being responsible for the death of his son two years earlier in a car crash. Colyn Bedale-Taylor had been heartbroken at the death of his son, nineteen-year-old Digby, in a motor accident in 1982. It was well-known in the village that he spent long periods of time sat alone next to his son's headstone in the graveyard of St James's Church.

However, according to Graham Backhouse, events then escalated dramatically. Bedale-Taylor then told Backhouse he was responsible for planting the car bomb in the Volvo, and had intended to kill the man he believed was responsible for his son's death. He then produced a Stanley knife and attacked Backhouse who, despite being badly injured, ran back along the passageway and grabbed his shotgun, which had been nearby. He raised the shotgun and warned his neighbour that he would shoot unless he put the knife down. Bedale-Taylor ignored the warning and attacked Backhouse again with the open blade of the knife. As the two men struggled, Backhouse told detectives, he had no choice but to shoot his attacker,

'I ran into the hallway and grabbed a gun; Bedale-Taylor was still after me. I shouted I had got a gun but he still kept coming and I shot him. He fell back and I shot him again and that was it.'

With Bedale-Taylor now dead, Backhouse had activated the alarm system and collapsed by the kitchen door to await the emergency services.

Graham Backhouse was taken to Frenchay Hospital and received eighty stitches to the deep cuts on his face, which ran from his ear to his chin. He was placed under immediate armed guard, alongside his wife who was still recovering from the effects of the car bomb. The police were taking no more chances with the Backhouses' safety, following another attempt on their lives.

With the farmer and his wife safely protected by armed officers, it was now time for detectives and forensic officers to piece together exactly what took place at Widden Hill Farm.

Right from the outset, something about Graham Backhouse's story did not seem quite right to the detectives. Detective Superintendent Tom Evans, who had taken charge of the investigation, asked forensic officers to scour the farm and outbuildings, while detectives sifted carefully through the house itself. As they did so, more and more anomalies were uncovered in Backhouse's story. Firstly, it was discovered that Graham Backhouse had asked his wife not to drive her own Fiat to the vets that morning; telling her that the ignition was faulty, and giving her the keys to his Volvo instead. Secondly, came the all-important question of the farmer's finances. It appeared that Backhouse's dairy farm was in severe debt to the tune of £70,000 (today's equivalent of almost £320,000). Yet, despite his cashflow problems he had recently doubled his wife's life insurance policy from £50,000 to £100,000 (worth approximately £450,000 today). Had the elaborate car bombing been a deliberate plan to murder his own wife, rather than an assassination attempt on the farmer himself?

Yet there was still the question of the numerous death threats, not to mention the attempt on Backhouse's life by Colyn Bedale-Taylor. Tom Evans decided to dig a little deeper.

Pathologist Dr William Kennard was asked to give his view on the wounds sustained to the two men. He stated that, in his professional opinion, for the farmer's chest wound to have been inflicted by another person, Backhouse would have needed to have been stood perfectly still, neither resisting or raising his hands in any form of self-defence, nor moving backwards. Dr Kennard considered this virtually impossible, especially taking into account Backhouse's version of events.

Secondly, although the Stanley knife had been in Colyn Bedale-Taylor's hand, his own blood, from the shotgun wound he had received, was underneath the knife. This seemed impossible if, as Backhouse claimed, he had inflicted the wound on the farmer *before* being shot. Remember, the farmer claimed that he had only shot Bedale-Taylor *after* his assailant had attacked him with the knife.

Home Office crime scene expert Geoffrey Robinson also cast doubt over the legitimacy of the crime scene. Blood spatters on the floors and walls of a violent crime scene, always fall in a characteristic 'exclamation mark' style pattern. In contrast to this distinctive trait usually found at crime scenes, the blood on the floors at Widden Hill Farm had fallen in round splashes; this strongly suggested that Backhouse had been standing still and the blood had simply dripped onto the floor.

In addition, several items of furniture had been knocked over, apparently during the struggle (according to Backhouse). However, some of the furniture had landed on top of Mr Bedale-Taylor's blood. If, as Graham Backhouse claimed, he had shot his attacker only *after* the two men had struggled and he had been stabbed, his blood could not have been underneath the furniture. This seemed to indicate that tables and chairs had been deliberately pushed over *after* the event to create the impression of a struggle, and that the knife wound must have been inflicted only after this had occurred, rather than before. To further strengthen this theory, blood from Backhouse's left hand was smeared on one of these fallen chairs, yet there was no blood on the gun. If, as Backhouse had claimed, he had only picked up the gun and fired it *after* being stabbed, surely some traces of blood would have transferred onto the grip and trigger of the shotgun.

This was enough for detectives to formally question Graham Backhouse. Nevertheless, a competent lawyer could easily dismiss these anomalies, claiming that his client had simply become confused over the sequence of events; hardly surprising for someone who had suffered such a traumatic experience.

However, Detective Superintendent Tom Evans felt certain of Backhouse's guilt. He ordered his detectives to dig deeper into the case. It was not long until two more crucial pieces of information came to light.

Officers had been unable to identify the obviously disguised handwriting on the 'YOU NEXT' note left with the impaled lamb's head. Then, police document specialist Mike Hall noticed the very faint impression of a doodle on the corner of the piece of paper used to write the note. Detectives then found a matching doodle in a notebook in a kitchen drawer at Backhouse's farm. It appeared that Backhouse had taken a piece of paper from his own notebook to create the threatening letter. Officers also noticed a brown woollen fibre clinging to the threatening letter, which matched one of Backhouse's own sweaters.

Perhaps most chillingly of all, a search of police files uncovered that Backhouse had a previous criminal conviction.

Eleven years earlier, in 1973, he had been tried (along with his father) for cattle rustling. Both men had been fined, with the judge telling Backhouse he was 'both disgraceful and dishonourable'. It seemed that Graham Backhouse had a track record of resorting to crime when in financial difficulties.

Backhouse was arrested and formally charged on 14th May with the attempted murder of his wife and the murder of his neighbour. When asked to respond, he replied 'Not guilty. It was self-defence.' Margaret Backhouse, still recovering in hospital, also refused to believe her husband had attempted to kill her.

However, there was to be yet another twist in the tale. With Backhouse on remand in Horfield Prison, the editor of the *Bristol Evening Post* received a letter claiming that Backhouse 'was NOT the bomber' and claiming that 'Mr Bedale-Taylor was responsible.' Unbeknown to Graham Backhouse, the police had intercepted the letter. It would transpire that he had offered a fellow inmate £2,000 to smuggle the letter out of prison on his behalf. Unfortunately for Backhouse, forensic tests on the letter indicated that it matched the handwriting on the threatening letters Backhouse had received at the farm.

It now seemed an open-and-shut case. Nevertheless, Backhouse's thirteen-day trial at Bristol Crown Court during February of 1985 was not to be without its drama. The accused man stood in the dock, heavily scarred about the face. His wife sat in court too, with crutches by her side. The public gallery was packed, and the nation's media watched on.

James Black Q.C., prosecuting for the Crown, claimed that Backhouse 'had overegged the pudding' and 'thought himself to be more intelligent than the police.' The prosecution contended that Backhouse had placed the knife in Bedale-Taylor's hand after shooting him. It was also revealed that

Backhouse had carved the initials 'CBT' onto the handle of the red Stanley knife. Yet a search of the other 500 tools owned by Colyn Bedale-Taylor showed that none of them bore his initials.

Home office forensic experts meticulously rebuilt the car bomb from the wreckage and were able to demonstrate that Backhouse had easy access to all the ingredients at his farm, including a makeshift detonator, shotgun cartridges, electric wiring, and steel piping. Despite Backhouse claiming he had been slashed with the Stanley knife before opening fire, there was not a single trace of his blood on the shotgun. Medical experts were introduced to testify that his wounds were almost certainly self-inflicted. The accused man's attempts to blame others were dismissed, and the jury was reminded of the recent increase in Maggie's life insurance.

Yet, despite this weight of circumstantial and forensic evidence, Backhouse still maintained his innocence. His defence counsel described him as a devoted family man who loved Maggie and their two children. Even his wife did not think him capable of having committed such horrific crimes; and the defence argued that he did not possess the technical capability to have constructed a car bomb. In fact, Backhouse was known to be technically inept. This revelation was further enforced by expert witness Dr Alexander Grant who testified that 'whoever planted the bomb which injured Mrs Backhouse would have needed a high degree of technical knowledge and expertise.'

Yet, all the defence needed to secure an acquittal for their client would be to create enough doubt in the minds of jurors. Would Backhouse's protestations of innocence prove sufficient? In another extraordinary development, events were to take an unexpected and dramatic turn on the twelfth day of the trial.

It was revealed in court that Margaret Backhouse had received a threatening letter which seemed to implicate someone else in the car bombing attempt; seemingly the husband of a woman who had been involved with the accused man:

'I won't make the same mistake this time. He's got to suffer like I did. You got to die, Maggie, believe me I'm not fooling.'

Handwriting expert Mike Hall testified in court that Graham Backhouse had not written the note. He had been under careful watch in prison since his first attempt to smuggle a letter to the *Bristol Evening Post*.

The next dramatic twist in the tale on day twelve of the proceeding sparked a public panic and a major bomb alert. Prosecuting counsel James Black Q.C. reported that the wiring on his Volvo car (a similar model to that belonging to Graham Backhouse) had been tampered with during the course of the trial. The bomb squad were called in to ensure the barrister's car was safe and to seal off the building adjacent to the parked car, Fairfax House. Doubt in the accused man's guilt was now beginning to creep into the minds of the jurors. With Backhouse under lock and key, who else could have tampered with James Black's car? Perhaps Backhouse was not guilty after all? With the defence's case complete, it would now be left to the eight-man and four-woman jury to decide.

The jury deliberated for five and a half hours before finally returning their verdict. By a majority of 10 – 2, Backhouse was found guilty of the murder of Colyn Bedale-Taylor and guilty of the attempted murder of his wife, Maggie. He gripped the handrails of the dock, sighed, and looked towards the heavens as he was given two concurrent life sentences. His wife showed no outward sign of emotion as he was led away. Neither one looked at the other.

In June 1994, Graham Backhouse suffered a fatal heart

attack while playing cricket at Grendon Underwood Prison near Aylesbury, England. He was fifty-three years old. Following his death, it was revealed that while in prison he had become engaged to marry Rosemary Aberdour, a con artist who was serving two years in prison for stealing £3 million from the charitable foundation at the National Hospital for Neurology Development, by posing as a titled aristocrat.

Margaret Backhouse died peacefully in her sleep in March 1995. She was aged only forty-eight.

In a strange twist, it transpired that James Black Q.C., who had prosecuted Backhouse during the trial and whose car had been tampered with, had been the same barrister who had unsuccessfully defended him eleven years earlier during his court appearance for cattle rustling.

However, three nagging questions remained unanswered. Who posted the threatening letter to Mrs Backhouse during the trial? Her husband could not have done so. How did the technically inept farmer manage to construct such an effective car bomb? And, perhaps most mysteriously of all, who tampered with James Black's car?

Did Graham Backhouse have an accomplice? Did a shadowy second party escape justice? We will probably never know.

ACKNOWLEDGEMENTS AND REFERENCES

This book would not have been possible without the continued encouragement and help of Kevin & Jayne Ramage. Thank you for your enduring support. I would also like to express my gratitude to Ellen McBride, Alexa Reid, the M Shed Museum, Bristol Archives, the National Archives in Kew, Bath History Group, Bristol Radical History Group, Bristol Museum, Cinema Treasures, Alfie Skinner, The Central Criminal Court at the Old Bailey, Lloyds Shipping, St Mary's Church, Bitton, Horfield Prison, Records of the GWR, the FBI, Harvard University, *Police Gazette*, Wales News Service, Lloyds of London, Christchurch, Hanham, The Internet Movie Database, National Churches Trust, Bristol and Avon Family History Society, Mark Coath-Wilson, National Library of Australia, Box People and Places, Bank of England, Avon and Somerset Police, Shepton Mallet Prison Archives, Somerset Council Archives, BBC News archives, Yale University USA, History of Bath Research Group, Bath Historical Directories, Dave Backwith, Roger Ball,

The following newspapers, journals, books, and other sources of information have also been invaluable in either helping to piece together the stories contained in this book, or for kindly supplying their permission for the reproduction of information:

Avon and Somerset Police Archives, Ancestry.com, *San Francisco Call and Post, Western Daily Press, Bristol Times and Mirror*, Odeon Cinemas, capitalpunishment.org, Hansard Archives (House of Commons), Gloucestershire Police Archives, the British Newspaper Archive, DC Thomson, Newspapers.com, Exeter Crown Court, Genuki, Judiciary UK, National Asylum Records Kew, *Western Daily Press, The Times, Daily Telegraph, Chard and Ilminster News, Bedfordshire Mercury, Central Somerset Gazette, Daily Herald, Phrenographic Register, Bristol Mercury, British Medical Journal, Bristol Evening Post, The Law Journal, Sunday Pictorial, Daily Mail, Daily Mirror, Journal Times, Tennessee Daily News Journal, Dundee Courier, FindMyPast, UK Census Records 1851 – 1921, Bath Chronicle, Somerset Live, Edinburgh Evening News, Illustrated Police News, Western Gazette, Folkstone Chronicle, Birmingham Mail, Sunday Mirror,* The True Crime Archive, Medium.com, Unsolved Murders UK Archive, Hansard 1803 – 2005, The Colt Manufacturing Company USA,

BIBLIOGRAPHY OF PUBLISHED RESOURCES USED

Nicotiana Brittanica, by Will Simpson and Jim McNeill, *Somerset and Bristol Murder Stories,* by Neil Walden, *Bristol Danger, Death and Dark Deeds,* by Cynthia Stiles, *A Shocking History of Bristol,* by Derek Robinson, *More Bristol Murders,* by Nicola Sly, *St Mary's Church, Bitton, A Brief History,* by Bob Willis, *The Cock Road Gang,* by Ian S. Bishop, *Foul Deeds and Suspicious Deaths in Bath,* by Kirsten Elliot, *A History of Mendip Cave Rescues & Incidents,* by Alan Gray, *Oxford Dictionary of National Biography*, *The Bristol Riots* (1974), by Susan Thomas, *The 1831 Reform Riots in Bristol* (Bristol Museums Publication), *Social Reform in Britain*, by E. Mellen, *Bristol Past and Present*, by J.F. Nicholls and John Taylor, *Bread or Batons?: Unemployed Workers' Struggles in 1930s Bristol* by Dave Backwith and Roger

Ball, *The Port of Bristol*, by Andy King, *Lost Bristol*, by Victoria Coules, *Bristol: A People's History*, by Peter Aughton, *Culture & Imperialism*, by Edward W. Said, *The History of Common Law*, by Sir Matthew Hales, *Commentaries on the Laws of England, by William Blackstone, A History of the 20th Century*, by Martin Gilbert,

Companion books to *Bristol: Bullets, Blades & Barricades* also by Mark Bridgeman

The Scottish Murder Book
14 Fascinating real-life murder trials
from Perthshire, Angus, and Fife
Available in paperback and ebook
£9.99

The Dark Side of the Dales
Tales of murder and mystery from the Yorkshire Dales
Available in paperback & ebook (new expanded edition)
£9.99

Nothing For Something: The Violet Charlesworth Story
The story of the Edwardian con artist
who fooled the world - three times
Published by Whittles Publishing Ltd
£18.99

The Lost Village of Lawers
Perthshire's 'lost' and abandoned village, famous for
its enigmatic location on the shores of Loch Tay,
and for the legend of 'The Lady of Lawers'.
Available in paperback and ebook
£8.99

The River Runs Red - New Edition
True Stories of Murder, Mystery and Deception
from Highland Perthshire's Dark Past.
£10.99

Mark's titles are available from all good bookshops, online retailers, or via www.markbridgemanauthor.co.uk

Free Sample

Nothing For Something: The Violet Charlesworth Story

Chapter 1: The Bait

This story begins with a mystery and ends with a riddle.

Illuminated only by the bright moonlight of a chilly January night, a young man dressed in a slightly dishevelled chauffeur's uniform, and a well-dressed young lady about 35 years of age staggered from the scene of a motor-car accident and lay down on the side of the empty highway, momentarily gathering their thoughts. The New Year festivities had recently passed; it was now a few minutes before 9 pm on 2 January 1909, a crisp, still, and crystal-clear Saturday evening. Seemingly still dazed, the pair glanced first left, then right, into the bluish hue of the moonlit night. They were quite alone. No streetlights illuminated that isolated stretch of road. A light was shining from a window of the Ship Inn, a few hundred yards to the east of them.

The narrow, twisting, and lonely coast road in North Wales on which the accident had occurred that evening ran like a thin, flat ribbon chiselled into the side of an otherwise dangerously steep cliff face, 50 feet above the rocks and sea below. The only protection for road users from the sleep drop and the jagged rocks beneath was afforded by a low stone wall approximately 18 inches thick and no more than 3 feet in height.

Above and behind the roadway, which had been carved, then levelled, from the craggy hillside, the moonlit hills and snow-frosted mountains of North Wales loomed ominously, casting a shadow across any passers-by, and thoughtlessly shedding the occasional loose shard of rock, allowing it to cascade downwards onto the surface of the road.

The accident had occurred close to the small community of Penmaenmawr, on the Bangor to Colwyn Bay road, at a sharp bend in the highway called Penmaenbach Point. This notoriously dangerous curve in the road sits close to an oddly shaped rock nicknamed the Devil's Thumb which, protruding from the base of the cliff, resembles a giant digit pointing portentously towards the sky. It appeared that the wheels of the unfortunate automobile, which had been motoring north-eastwards towards Conwy, had skidded, then hurtled into the low boundary wall that protected road users from the serrated rocks and tide-washed sands that sat threateningly below the road. At the precise point at which the motor car had come to rest, there was a two-foot-wide gap in the wall (designed to offer pedestrians a haven from traffic at the dangerous bend in the road). The car was sitting motionless with its engine still running, sandwiched at an angle inside this space; one of its narrow front wheels dangled precariously close to the edge of the precipice. The vehicle's rear wheels sat resting against the kerb, which had acted as a chock, preventing the motor car from rolling any further forward.

It was an extraordinary piece of bad luck that the driver of the motor car on that fateful evening had succeeded in skidding and crashing into the only point in the low, 18-inch-thick, stone sea wall in which there was a gap, and at which a vehicle would be least protected from the rocks and sea below. Nevertheless, the expensive imported Minerva motor car had somehow managed to wedge itself into the only gap on that particular stretch of road. Considering the damage sustained to the wall, the motor car did not appear to be too badly affected, and it had also miraculously avoided a collision with one of the many thick telegraph poles positioned at intervals of 50 yards or so along the side of the roadway.

Despite the relative quietness of the highways in 1909, driving was a much more trying occupation for the individual than it is today. Country roads were not often metalled. Nor were they helpfully lined with reflective white paint, or adorned with cats' eyes. No streetlighting illuminated the driver's journey, and vehicle headlights were little more than the oil-lit carriage lights that had previously adorned horse-drawn modes of transportation. Steering was cumbersome and unresponsive (compared to that on a modern vehicle) and braking systems relied on the external 'cable and drum' method, which was susceptible to the vagaries of extreme weather. The Bangor to Colwyn Bay stretch of road has since been widened and altered, to become the modern A55 North Wales Expressway, and is barely recognisable when compared to its appearance in 1909. Now a busy dual carriageway, the modern road is complemented by crash barriers and streetlighting. It is hard to imagine the much narrower and unmetalled road surface that would have challenged the Edwardian motorist. Coupled with the absence of any warning signs, far less powerful headlights, and the extreme darkness, driving conditions in the Edwardian era would seem exacting indeed to any modern motorist.

Automobiles were still a comparatively rare sight, certainly in North Wales, and particularly such an expensive and fine example of the motor car as the imported Belgian Minerva 1908 Landaulette.

Yet earlier in the day the shiny, bottle-green Minerva, registration number LB 6709, had certainly turned heads as it sped from St Asaph, through

Colwyn Bay, Conwy, and onwards to Bangor, as it conveyed its three occupants on their Saturday afternoon excursion. If you were affluent enough to own a motor car, it was a toy of pleasure, to be used for driving as fast as possible, for feeling the wind in your hair, and for attracting the envious (and frequently disapproving) glances of pedestrians as you sped by. With its removable landau cover, the Minerva offered its owner the perfect driving experience, a chance to see and be seen in pleasant weather, yet providing a modicum of protection from the elements. The Minerva marque also offered its owner a high level of build quality; at that time it was considered second only to Rolls Royce as the ultimate in motoring status symbols. Vehicle prices in 1909 reflected this, the cost of an average motor car matching that of a small house. Recent purchasers of the Minerva marque in 1908 had included the kings of Belgium, Sweden, and Norway, the American business tycoon Henry Ford, and the Belgian Impressionist artist Anna Boch.

On that chilly but clear January day in 1909, this gleaming example of the Minerva motor car had left St Asaph carrying its three occupants for a day's excursion to Bangor, followed by afternoon tea at the Castle Hotel, concluding with a 20-mile nocturnal return drive. In the car were the chauffeur, 25-year-old Albert Watts, and his employers, Lillian and Violet Charlesworth. Lillian was 35 and a little reserved. Her sister, Violet, was 24 (in fact, that evening's motor-car accident would occur just a few days prior to Violet's 25th birthday), and the more flamboyant of the two siblings. Violet was dressed luxuriously; she regularly purchased lavish outfits from the high-class Brook Street fashion houses in London. She adorned herself in expensive jewellery and sported a large and very noticeable full-length crimson motor coat of the type to keep stylish young ladies warm while they travelled the country in their motor cars. Violet's fashion sense was keen, as was her wit and sense of business. Yet within the strict social order of Edwardian England, with its limited opportunities for unchaperoned liaisons, Violet Charlesworth still managed to attract many admirers and much comment (some complimentary, some derogatory). Not only did she live an active and public love life; she also dabbled in stocks and shares on that strictly male preserve, the London Stock Exchange, for which she retained the services of her own broker.

Despite employing not one but two chauffeurs, Violet generally insisted on driving her own motor car, particularly during the hours of darkness. She enjoyed the exhilaration of night-time driving. Although in 1903 the national speed limit had been increased from 14 to 20 mph, this was not sufficient for Violet, who preferred to drive much faster whenever the situation allowed. In truth, there was little chance of being apprehended or prosecuted on the quiet country roads of Britain, and the speed limits, largely unenforceable, were generally ignored. Her desire to be seen behind the wheel often saw her suffer the sharp backlash of local opinion and comment (perhaps tinged with a little jealousy too) as she powered along the highways and byways of Britain. It was widely thought in 1909 that women did not possess the correct temperament for driving, a skill much better suited to the logical and more rational male mind. Indeed, the driver's position in the car was often the most uncomfortable, frequently exposed to the elements, and not considered suitable for the 'more delicate' sex. The attitude to female motorists of the Edwardian era can be perfectly summed up in a commonly used disparaging remark of the time, often shouted by male bystanders to a lady motorist in her vehicle – 'Woman at the wheel!'

It was not long, however, before the rigorous social etiquette of the era caught up with the new trend for female motoring, and instruction was given to ladies, informing them how to dress appropriately when inside a motor car. And if they insisted on taking the wheel themselves, 'helpful' advice was readily provided.

Violet soon became one of the first female applicants for the new Licence to Drive a Motor Vehicle, as required under the terms of the 1903 Motor Car Act.

Meanwhile, at the scene of the accident at Penmaenbach Point, the slightly dazed and confused Lillian recovered her composure first, and helped Albert to his feet. She staggered the few hundred yards along the road in her full-length dress and coat, and threw open the door of The Ship. Obviously distressed, she blurted out the terrible news: 'There has been a dreadful car accident! My younger sister has been catapulted into the sea.'

The occupants of the Ship Inn, mostly quarrymen and fishermen, followed her outside into the cold night air. One of the fisherman ran along the Morfa to Penmaenbach Cottages to request help, while the rest made their way quickly westward, towards the scene of the accident.

In addition to the occupants of The Ship, it was not long before a small crowd of people gathered, all curious and anxious to help. Albert explained that Lillian's sister Violet had wanted to drive – in fact, he claimed, she had insisted on doing so. After the trio had departed the Castle Hotel in Bangor for their return journey to St Asaph, Albert had climbed into the passenger seat, and Violet had taken the wheel. However, as the car had rounded the sharp bend in the road next to the Devil's Thumb, it had struck a loose stone and skidded violently through 90 degrees, before colliding with the wall. According to Lillian's version of events the violent and sudden jolt had catapulted a screaming Violet over the open-top glass windscreen down the cliff face, and into the sea below. In the Minerva, it was only the rear passenger compartment that was protected by the landau cover; the front seats were exposed to the elements.

As the small group listened in horror to Albert's story, Lillian frantically implored them to help her search for Violet. In the pitch-black of the night, Lillian said, she had heard her sister scream, before the sickening sound of a splash as Violet had hit the water. In just a matter of moments, Lillian explained, she feared that Violet's body might have been washed away.

Increasingly, more people arrived. The local police constable, PC Evans from Penmaenmawr, was called, and an initial search for Violet was organised. Meanwhile, Superintendent Rees and Sergeant Evans were summoned.

After hastily requisitioning a horse and cart they soon arrived at the scene to join the worried group, who were all perched by the low wall, peering down to the reflection of the moonlight on the shoreline below. In 1909 serious motor-car accidents were still a rare occurrence on Britain's roads; accidents involving a stray horse and cart were still a far more frequent occurrence. On the rare occasion that collisions involving motor cars did occur, the low speeds attainable at that time usually reduced the chance of any serious injury. In fact, during the whole of the previous year there had only been a total of 16 motor-car accidents recorded on Britain's roads. Violet Charlesworth's accident was the first such incident ever investigated by the Conwy Police.

Dr Moreton Roberts was asked to examine the two survivors. At this point Lillian Charlesworth was now lying in a slumped and incoherent manner on the ground near the location of the accident; she seems to have regressed into this strange pattern of behaviour despite having been well enough to run to The Ship a few minutes earlier. Albert was at that moment leaning against the low wall and attempting to describe the events of the evening to PC Evans.

After examining Lillian and Albert, Roberts described them both as appearing to be 'cold, bruised and almost insensible, and not able to offer a coherent explanation'.

Lillian, he explained later, 'was not injured, only apparently suffering from shock. Both she and the chauffeur were in much distress; however, they are in no worse plight than that. I then went in search of her sister's body with the others.'

Albert only constantly repeated the same question: 'Where is the lady? Where is she?'

Instead of proceeding with their questioning, the police decided to escort the pair to the nearby Gwynfa Lodging House, a large property on the hilly Paradise Crescent in Penmaenmawr, in order that they might rest for the night. The landlady had spare rooms available, and lit a fire for the pair. 'Interviewing can resume in the morning,' explained Rees, first making sure he had obtained some identification from the two survivors.

Although hampered by the darkness, the police conducted a thorough search of the rocky shoreline below the site of the crash, but were still unable to locate Violet's body. This appeared to confirm the survivors' story that Violet had been 'catapulted' into the waters of the Menai Strait and ultimately to her death. The decision was taken to postpone any further search until the morning of 3 January, when daylight would better suit their efforts.